A GUIDE TO THE ME

by

Eric Overton

LOCAL HISTORY PUBLICATIONS

Published by
Local History Publications
316 Green Lane
Streatham
London SW16 3AS

© Mary Overton 1994

ISBN 1 873520 07 7

The Medieval Manor

Within his chamber weak and dying,
While the Norman Baron lay,
Loud, without, his men were crying,
"Shorter hours and better pay!"
Anon 19th century.

When studying the medieval manorial system it is important to remember that the manor, the village and the parish were not necessarily synonymous units. In practice a manor could consist of one village or several - or, in some instances, none at all! Conversely villages sometimes serviced one manor and sometimes several. Some manors were coextensive with the area of one ecclesiastical parish, while other manorial estates contained several such parishes each with its own church. The only consistent thing about the manorial system was its inconsistency.

Notwithstanding the above, the manorial system is best envisaged by imagining an ideal manor consisting of a village and a parish church, held by a Lord of the Manor who dwelt in a manor house standing in its own grounds. The land containing the manor house was the Lord's own personal part of the manor reserved for his exclusive use and was called the 'demesne lands.' These usually consisted of the best arable and meadow land in the district and provided an important part of the Lord's livelihood. The demesne was usually enclosed by walls or fences.

The villeins and other serfs of the manor lived in the village. They dwelt in small houses, placed side by side, each house having a small enclosed plot of land at the rear called a 'close'. Within, or close to, the village was the parish church, which stood in its own land. The incumbent priest was also granted a piece of land for his own use called the 'glebe land,' the 'church furlong' or the 'parson's close.'

Our imaginary manor, then, was composed of the Lord of the Manor's demesne lands; the village; the parish church that stood in its own land; the glebe land, church furlong or parson's close; and the communal manor lands, utilised on a more or less communal basis by the villeins for their own needs, and comprising arable fields, meadows, commons, wastelands and woodlands.

The Lands of the Manor

To obtain some idea as to the layout of our hypothetical manor it is best to imagine walking from the centre of the village towards the outer limits of the estate. Firstly, adjoining or close to the village, several enclosed meadows would be seen. Immediately beyond these meadows would stretch the open country which, at first, would consist of three large unfenced fields of arable land.

Next, on the way outwards, was the uncultivated pasture lands - the commons. Beyond this, stretching to the outer limits of the manor, were the wastelands, woodlands and forest.

The essence of the manorial system was that the Lord of the Manor allowed the villeins to cultivate portions of the communal arable land, graze their animals on the commons, root their hogs on the waste and take timber and fuel from the woodlands. In return for these grants the villeins paid rent and were bound to cultivate the Lord's demesne lands for him, pasture his animals and perform many other services - a bargain if you were the Lord of the Manor.

The Arable Land

The arable land was divided into three great unfenced fields known as the 'common fields.' These fields were each divided into a number of large divisions called furlongs, shots, dells and various other names. Each of the furlongs was sub-divided into strips (or selions), with each strip separated from the others by raised baulks of unploughed land. The strips ran parallel to each other over the full length of each furlong and usually contained between half and one acre of land. At right angles to the strips, at each end of the furlong, ran the 'headlands' - unploughed lanes giving access to all the strips in the furlong and to the other furlongs of the great field.

The villeins each held a number of these strips of the 'common fields' at rent from the Lord of the Manor. The actual number of strips held varied from person to person. Each villein's total land holding was so divided that he held exactly one third of the total in each great field. By ancient custom, probably dating back to Saxon times, the strips held by any individual villein were never located in one convenient block. The essence of this ancient principle was that the strips were of comparatively small size and well scattered all over the common fields.

The term 'the common fields' suggests a co-operative system of farming and, although there is evidence of individual enterprise, communal methods were widely used for at least some of the time, especially at ploughing, haymaking and harvest. The common fields were usually cultivated according to ancient custom, or at least the general consent of the villeins. Everyone had to conform to this and individual choice of crops was only possible in a villein's 'close' which adjoined his home.

When the Lord's demesne lands needed ploughing, the villeins co-operated with each other and yoked their animals with those of their neighbours in order to provide the necessary plough-teams for the purpose. This ploughing and other tasks on the demesne, such as mowing the Lord's hay or reaping his corn, was accomplished by communal effort. Because of this co-operation it is often assumed that the villeins used similar combined efforts to cultivate the common fields as this would, without doubt, have been the most efficient way of working.

Evidence of various encroachments and disputes between villeins can be found in most manorial court rolls and seems to suggest that communal working, far from being a universal practice, was more often seasonal, temporary, and a matter for agreement between neighbours.

The manorial system was extremely inefficient and exacted an extremely heavy toll from its workers. For instance, a villein holding thirty acres would find it distributed over thirty strips scattered over all three common fields of his village. The waste of time and effort which resulted from these piecemeal holdings is not hard to imagine.

Over the years the holdings in the common fields became even more complicated due to the sub-division of the original holdings to accommodate the descendants of the original villeins. By this process the individual holdings tended to get smaller and, in many cases, communal cultivation of the common fields became the only feasible method of working. The harvests in such cases were gathered co-operatively and shared out in proportion to the size of the holdings. Some of the more enlightened Lords of the Manor, by agreement with their villeins, effected reform by consolidating the manorial holdings into fewer strips. This increased efficiency by reducing the time spent by the villeins in getting round their holdings in the common fields.

The Meadows

These were situated close to the village often adjoining the great 'common fields,' but unlike the latter they were fenced for part of the year. The meadows were some times called the 'Lammas lands,' which no doubt explains the widespread use of Lammas as a road name! Lammas was the name for the first day of August which was formerly observed as a harvest festival day.

The meadows were a vital part of the village economy, and they were carefully enclosed after Christmas until the crop of grass was taken from them in the late summer. They were under the protection of a manorial official, the hayward, who saw that the fences were not broken and impounded any animals that strayed into the meadows during the growing period and presented their owners at the Manorial Court.

The meadows were some times called the 'Lammas lands,' which no doubt explains the widespread use of Lammas as a road name!

The meadows were held in common by the villeins, each of whom was allocated a portion of the hay produced either by a system of rotation or the drawing of lots. Once the grass had been cut in the late summer, the meadows reverted to common grazing land until the next enclosure.

This principle was also applied to the arable land, on which the holder alone had the right to the crop, but after the harvest had been gathered the common fields became common grazing until the next ploughing time.

These 'rights of common' were one of the most valuable of the villeins rights and enabled him to use not only the uncultivated pastures and wastelands - the 'commons' of popular speech - but also the cultivated arable fields and meadows once the crops had been harvested.

The Commons, Wastelands and Woodlands

These lands were the next most important component of the manorial economy. 'Rights of common' were vital to the villeins because they relied on pasture to keep their plough beasts in good condition. The right of 'common of pasture' therefore was tenaciously guarded. However, this was not an unlimited right and in early times it was conferred only on those holding land in the common fields in proportion to the number of strips held.

The whole object of rights of common was to support and sustain manorial agricultural routine and, in early times, only those animals directly involved therein were 'commonable,' viz. horses and oxen for the plough and sheep and cows for manuring. Later the rights were extended to allow for the grazing of goats, swine and geese. Later still the rights were extended to include those who only held a 'close' or 'assart' of the Lord of the Manor. The 'assarts' and their effects are described later on.

Where the commons merged into the wastelands is difficult to say, the former being natural pasture land and the latter being covered by furze, bracken, trees and such. Some manors only had a limited common pasture which was strictly reserved for its own members. In other cases there were large tracts of waste between manors, often so vast in extent that no clear boundaries had ever been defined and they formed a sort of no-mans land in which the manors adjoining it inter-commoned at will. For example, the New Forest contained about 60,000 acres of wasteland which was fringed by some twenty one manors.

However, the waste was much more than extra pasturage for from it the villein obtained many things essential to his daily life. Most importantly it provided him with wood, a primary requisite. His house, farm implements and household utensils were mainly made of wood and he also relied on it almost entirely for fuel.

The villein's rights to take wood from the waste fell under three headings : 'fire-bote' allowed him to take as much wood for fuel as he could get 'by hook or by crook' - i.e. such timber as he could knock down from standing trees with a crook of scythe; 'house-bote' allowed him to cut down a set number of trees per year for house repairs; and 'hay-bote' gave him the right to take wood or thorns to make and repair the fences of the enclosed meadows.

The wastes also provided many other useful things. Turfs were cut for roofing sheds and making up the baulks in the common fields; clay was dug for mill dams and dykes; sand and gravel was taken for building purposes; bracken was cut for litter (animal bedding); reeds and sedges were taken from ponds and swamps for thatching; wild fruits and berries were gathered for the kitchen; and the villeins found many other valuable things to help them in their struggle to live.

Assarts and Assarting

On most manors there were some villeins, and others, to whom the Lord had granted rights to clear parts of the manorial wastelands for which a small yearly rent was payable for this privilege. These newly cleared plots, known as 'assarts,' were usually located near the edge of the manor adjoining the forests. On the 'assarts,' as in the 'closes' of their village houses, the holders were free to grow whatever crops they pleased. The assarts were no doubt a godsend to those families burdened with more children that their shares in the common fields could sustain.

There were some disadvantages to assart holding. The assart was often located at the edge of the manor, and the land was not broken into cultivation, so that it required constant hard work to reclaim it from the wilderness which was for ever waiting to snatch it back. Possession of an assart did not carry with it any communal privileges such as went with the holdings in the common fields. It did not give a man the right to put any extra beasts on the common nor was the yearly rent relaxed when its holder served in an official capacity in the manor court, as were his other manorial dues and services. The assart was an extra and had to bear its own burdens.

Such then was the world of the medieval peasants - a far from easy one. Of course conditions varied greatly from manor to manor. Some manors were capable of providing better livings than others. Some Lords were benevolent, by the standards of the day, but most screwed every last advantage they could get out of their serfs.

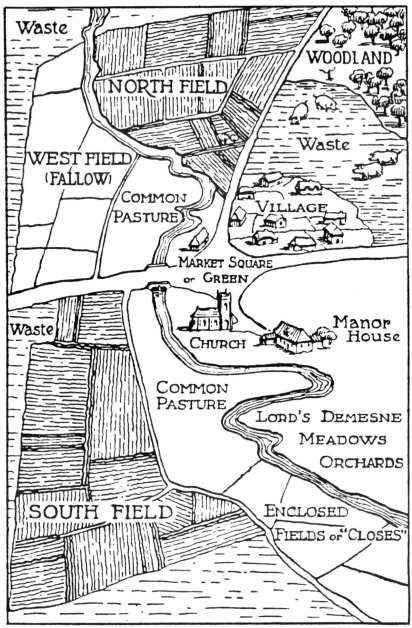

Waste

WOODLAND

NORTH FIELD

Waste

WEST FIELD
(FALLOW)

COMMON
PASTURE

VILLAGE

MARKET SQUARE
or GREEN

Waste

CHURCH

Manor
House

COMMON
PASTURE

LORD'S DEMESNE
MEADOWS
ORCHARDS

SOUTH FIELD

ENCLOSED
FIELDS or "CLOSES"

THE LAYOUT OF A "TYPICAL" MANOR IN THE MIDDLE AGES

This shows the three field rotation system of agriculture, with one field left
fallow (the west field) and the other two fields (the north and south fields)
divided into strips for cultivation, together with the Lord's demesne lands,
the commons, wastelands, woodlands, and the enclosed fields or closes.

The Manorial Population

It is a temptation to think of the manorial population as consisting only of serfs (the villeins) or freemen. This is an over-simplification and such a classification is more legal than practical. In fact there were many grades amongst both of these basic categories and many villeins were richer than the freemen.

Villeins, Serfs and Freemen

The villein's status was usually inherited by having been born of parents who were villeins. They were bound to the land they were born on and, in effect, part of the manorial assets to be bought and sold with it. Those who, with the Lord's permission, had settled on the manor of their own accord were classed as 'freemen.' The difference between the two was that the villein was tied to the land and could not legally leave it without the Lord's permission. On the other hand a 'freeman' could go as and when he pleased.

The mere fact of being classified a 'freemen' did not denote any material superiority to the villeins. In practice many 'freemen' only possessed an acre or two of land, and their only hope of keeping body and soul together was to seek extra employment. This was very often found on the holding of one of the despised villeins, some of whom held more land than they could cultivate without help! Thus the 'freeman's' legal liberty amounted to little more than a right to stop working when ever he pleased, with the knowledge that no one could compel him to start again. However, since the alternative to working was starvation his freedom was somewhat notional.

Pytel Holders

Much more important than the technical differences between 'freeman' and 'serf' were the many practical sub-divisions which existed among the servile population. The most prestigious of the serfs were those villeins holding 60 acres ('full lands') in the common field, followed by those holding 'half lands' of 30 acres. Others had to be content with 'fardels' or 'furlongs' of 10 and 15 acres. After these, at the lowest end of the social order, came the cotters, crofters and others who had no share in the common fields and eked out a living as best as they could from the small 'closes' of an acre or two attached to their small houses. They are sometimes described collectively as 'pytel-holders,' a 'pytel' being a small enclosed field.

The 60 acre holder, who owed his Lord manifold rents and services, was in a different class to a poor 'pytel-holder' who perhaps rendered a couple of hens a year, or did a days work on the demesne at harvest time, in sole payment for his holding.

Yet in the Manor Court or the King's Courts both were equal because both men had the 'stain of serfdom' and could not appeal against their Lords in the King's Courts. However, a 'freeman' could seek a legal remedy against his Lord's injustice in the King's Courts - in theory at least!

These differences in status between the serfs were both recognised and fully exploited by the Lords of the Manor. The larger the serf's holding the greater were the services demanded of him. In the Manor Courts, the larger holders were the first to be chosen to serve as jurors and were consistently given wider responsibilities than the smaller holders. They were required to provide their own plough-teams to work on the demesne, while the lesser holders were allowed to pool their teams for this purpose. At harvest time on the demesne the largest holders provided the carts and horses for carrying services and acted as overseers walking or riding about the demesne with white wands of office.

The lesser serfs also served on the demesne, on a descending scale, according to the size of their holdings and available equipment. At the lowest social level the crofters and cotters - the 'pytel-holders' - formed a real and very important social dividing line. Many of them were technically 'freemen' and others were serfs. However, their holdings had certain features in common :-

- ❑ They had no holdings in the common fields and were therefore free from the demands of communal cultivation.

- ❑ Their 'crofts' and 'closes' were too small to sustain them and their families.

- ❑ The services demanded of them by the Lord, in keeping with the smallness of their 'closes,' were of a token nature and took up little of their time.

- ❑ They all needed more than could be produced by their land holding in order to live.

The only equipment these crofters and other small tenants had at their disposal were spades, hoes, mallets and suchlike and they were usually referred to in the manorial rolls, rather contemptuously, as 'poor men who work with their hands.' However, due to the above stated common factors, these various small-holding tenants provided a pool of readily available labour to all who could afford to pay for it. They were therefore a most important part of the economy of the medieval manor.

Villeins with 'full field' holdings, widows left with young families and unable to cope with their manorial obligations, villeins burdened with time consuming services and large holdings, as well as the Lords of the Manor themselves, were all ready enough to employ the small tenants. Without them life on the medieval manor would have been very much more difficult, if not impossible.

As the years passed, and the Lords of the Manor allowed ever more new lands to be 'assarted,' the numbers of these small tenants on the manor increased.

The Undermanni

These small tenants known collectively as 'undermanni,' became the farm labourers, ploughmen, herdsmen, carpenters, thatchers, smiths, weavers, wheelwrights, millers, coopers and so on and they were an essential part of manorial life. It was the 'undermanni' who, because of the lightness of their manorial obligations, were most easily able to persuade Lords of the Manor to commute such burdens for the payment of 'quit rents.' This left them almost free and, more importantly, also had the effect of prompting the villeins with common field holdings to obtain smaller commutations.

It must have been very irksome to a villein with a large holding, and burdened with many service obligations, to see the freedom enjoyed by many of those he considered his inferiors.

The 'undermanni' class of tenant, although holding only two or three acres, could cultivate whatever crops they wished in their own time and in their own way. Once they had finished work on their holdings they were free to turn their attention to other work for other masters and thus they prospered from the sale of their labours and enjoyed the profits.

The 'undermanni' were also able to experiment with crop production methods, and cultivated their small holdings in ways impossible to the villeins with common field holdings. The latter were bound to cultivate according to the custom of the manor and were also restricted by the demands of communal cultivation.

It is possible, therefore, that the 'undermanni' class of tenant was more important, and innovative of new working methods than is apparent from their scant treatment in the manorial records.

The gradual replacement of the villein's burdens and obligations by the payment of 'quit rents' was only possible because of the existence on the manors of the 'undermanni.'

It must have been very irksome to a villein with a large holding, and burdened with many service obligations, to see the freedom enjoyed by many of those he considered his inferiors.

As the tendency towards 'quit rents' proceeded the more necessary it became for the Lords of the Manor to be able to command a steady supply of labour for their various needs on the demesne lands. The 'quit rents' received paid the wages for such labourers and no doubt provided a cash surplus as well!

A Changing Population

The medieval manors were in a state of continual flux and change. The villeins with holdings in the common fields, especially the smaller holders who were burdened with large families were forced to do what they could to provide outlets for them. For this purpose they either purchased or rented 'assarts,' or took over extra cottages and plots within the village so as to accommodate their numerous offspring.

There was constant movement amongst the manorial tenantry. Some left their father's house to start life for themselves in some empty cottage and 'close,' or perhaps cleared an assart at the edge of the manorial waste and built a new house on it. Others preferred to seek a living by labour and engaged as ploughmen, carters or shepherds and served the Lord of the Manor on a full time basis for a fixed wage. There were also some who worked for other villeins who were unable or unwilling to operate their own holdings without assistance.

So, as we have seen, the manorial population was a complex and ever changing community. The comparatively secure life of the serfs, many of whom had quite large land holdings, contrasts strangely with many of the 'undermanni' who, although technically free, only had a mere 'pytel' and struggled to exist. Every manor was a world of change, and rising and falling fortunes, far from the ordered and unchanging entity pictured in the manorial records quoted in such books as 'The Victoria County History.' Conditions varied greatly between different districts. For example, manors in Yorkshire were mainly concerned with raising and tending sheep while the southern manors were mainly engaged with the plough, harrow and reap-hook.

Regardless of their many differences, the serf and his free brother on the manor also had much in common. Both were engaged in agriculture and the pastoral life, and both were subject to the demands of such pursuits. Much of the time of both was spent in the fields and on their 'closes.' Although many things separated them they were engaged on similar tasks.

The Years Work on the Manor

The 'typical' manor described earlier was operated on the 'three field' system. An alternative method of agriculture in general use in medieval times was the 'two field' system. In the latter system the manorial arable land was only divided into two great common fields one of which was cultivated whilst the other lay fallow. The following years the procedure was reversed and so each field was rested every alternate year.

The Three Field System

In the three field system the first great field was planted in the autumn with wheat or rye as the main crop. In the following spring a second field was planted with oats, barley or vetches (peas used for animal feed), while the third field remained fallow. The following year the fallow field was used for wheat, the first for oats, etc., while the second field lay fallow. In the third year the cycle was completed and thus each field was rested every third year.

In this elementary way the medieval villeins sought to maintain the fertility of the land. However, it was an almost impossible task because their crops were limited to wheat, oats, rye, barley, peas and beans. Since root vegetables and artificial grasses were unknown, any serious rotation of crops that would have given the ground a chance to recover was impossible. In this respect, as in many other matters, the villeins were as a great disadvantage.

Firstly, the Lords of the Manor, who had their own well fed animals which grazed on and manured the demesne lands, also claimed 'jus foldae' - i.e. the right to graze all the manorial sheep on his own lands for some part of each year. Secondly, the villeins were unable to keep very large numbers of animals of their own because of the difficulty of feeding them during winter and such animals as he did have got very scant winter rations. Thus the villeins had too few animals and were deprived of some of the benefit of those they did have. The resulting lack of manuring, together with ineffective crop rotation, resulted in minimal production in the common fields.

The Fallow Fields

A villein with a thirty acre holding in the common fields of our imaginary manor would have held ten acres in each great field. His ten acres in the fallow, together with the holdings of all the other villeins, were used as common grazing by them throughout the fallow year. Their animals, when not compelled to graze on the Lord's demesne, were kept on the fallow land in part to feed on its scanty vegetation, and in part to manure the ground. Each acre was considered capable of supporting at least two sheep. The fallow field was ploughed three times during its rest period. Firstly in April; then again in June, just deep enough to destroy the thistles; and finally in October when it was ploughed for the last time before the winter wheat was sown.

The Fields Under Cultivation

The other two fields took up much more of the villein's time. In January he started carting manure and marl (clay containing lime) to the fields ready to be ploughed in as soon as the weather was suitable. These were his means of fertilising the soil and were most important. His other means of conditioning the land was the straw from the previous year's harvest, which had been carefully stored under cover during the winter. This straw was mixed with earth and carted to the fields in early March and ploughed in.

In spring, the ploughing and harrowing, followed by the sowing of oats, barley, peas, beans or vetches, kept the villeins busy on their strips. Once all this was finished their labours in the common fields became less pressing and they were able to attend to the many secondary jobs that were waiting to be done. These included such matters as draining, ditching, and repair to the hedges surrounding their 'closes' and the enclosed meadows.

In April, the already mentioned first ploughing of the fallow field was duly carried out. The villeins also found many other jobs to do at this time, especially in their own 'closes' where they were free to grow such fruits and vegetables as were available to them.

Haymaking

In June, after the second ploughing of the fallow had been done, the haymaking called for a maximum communal effort. At this time the villeins had to give as many 'boon days' on the demesne meadows, as were necessary to complete the Lord of the Manor's haymaking. Only when this had been done were they able to make their own hay from the communal meadows which had been carefully enclosed and guarded for the purpose since Christmas. The villeins used long scythes for mowing and about an acre a day was cut.

After the haymaking the common field strips needed weeding, but this work was not usually started before St. John's Day (24th June) because country tradition asserted that weeds cut before that date would multiply threefold! The weeding was done with two long sticks, one held in the left hand had a forked end, while the other had a small curved blade. With these tools the villeins worked up and down their strips cleaning the corn of dock, thistle and other weeds. The women, at this time, gathered hemp and flax to be dried and spun into yarn for thread, rope and linen.

The Harvest

With the coming of August and the ripening harvest, the villein's activities reached their climax. The demands made upon them at this time by the Lords of the Manor were always extra heavy. For example, from August until Michaelmas (29th September), it was customary for them to do extra 'work days' on the demesne than at other times. However, even this was not enough and they also had to give as many 'boon days' as were necessary to safely gather in the Lord's harvest. The villein's entire family was pressed into service for this purpose and the work had absolute priority over all other matters.

The performance of their obligations to the Lords of the Manor must have made the gathering of their own harvests a very difficult and anxious business for the villeins. Their work load during these crucial weeks must have been almost endless. The wheat was cut with the sickle, or reap hook, and the ear was cut high up the stalk leaving the straw standing. Thus the sheaves were kept small for easy drying and cartage. The villeins, working in teams of five, cut about two acres of corn a day. The barley, oats, peas and beans were cut with the scythe.

Once the harvest had been gathered, and the wheat straw had been cut and stored, the heaviest part of the years work was over. The three common fields were now bare of crops and the animals were turned onto them to graze on the grass, weeds and stubble and provide manure. In October the animals on the field which had stood fallow during the past year were driven off and it was given its third and last ploughing prior to the sowing of the following year's wheat.

The villeins now started preparing for winter. They gathered and stored any available fruits and nuts; cut wood (and turfs and peat if available) for winter fuel; and vast amounts of bracken for bedding the animals was stored. The wheat straw, which had been stored, was used for thatching, as a supplement animal feed or bedding and the surplus was ploughed into the arable fields to rot and nourish the soil. In wet weather the villeins took the opportunity to thresh the corn. The Lords of the manor had this work done in their great barns but the villeins had to make do in a more cramped space, usually under a lean-to adjoining their cottages. After the threshing had been done the villeins no doubt estimated their gains from the year's work - if any!

Unfortunately there is no accurate way of assessing what these gains may have been. By studying the yields recorded on certain demesne lands, and allowing for the fact that most common field land was of much poorer quality, a reasonable estimate can be made. This indicates that a villein with a thirty acre holding of average quality probably produced from the twenty acres under cultivation (after the deduction of next year's seed corn, the church tithe, and the miller's 1/16th of the corn milled) 48 bushels of wheat, 66 of barley and 39 of oats, i.e. 153 bushels of mixed corn a year.

It has also been estimated that, circa 1260, the average yield for mixed corn was 11.5 bushels per acre. This required an initial 3.4 bushels of seed corn to produce and the miller received half a bushel as his grinding fee - i.e. a net yield of 7.5 bushels per acre. An indication of just how inefficient medieval farming was can be seen from the fact that around 1700 yields of 24 bushels per acre were being achieved, while in modern times yields in excess of 40 bushels per acre are common.

Studies indicate that an average medieval peasant family of five used approximately 36 bushels of corn per year. Our imaginary serf with his 30 acre holding therefore would have produced a comfortable surplus of corn. He would probably have used 36 bushels of his barley and oats to make bread, ale and porridge to feed his family and sold or exchanged the surplus of these crops, plus his 48 bushels of wheat, for cash or kind - wheaten bread would have been considered an unnecessary luxury!

It must be remembered that such a thirty acre holder was the aristocrat of the serfs and very much in a minority. Most villeins were worse off than this with fifteen acres or less. For them life was a struggle, which if the seasons were unkind, was often a losing one. For the 'pytel' holders with a mere two or three acres starvation was a real and ever present possibility, especially when a hard winter followed a poor harvest.

The Manorial Libestock

The resources of the villeins were not limited to their sacks of grain. They had other means of survival of which the most important were their animals. Their disadvantages in this respect have already been touched on but for the average villein the keeping of some livestock was vital. Of course actual numbers of the different species of animals kept varied with local needs and conditions.

Oxen were used all over England for ploughing and as draught animals. The use of horses for such purposes had increased after the Normans came but most landlords still considered the ox to be more economical because after a horse had served its purpose all that was left was its hide whereas the retired ox, after a short rest and a feed up, provided both its hide and food for the larder - life was too hard a struggle for sentiment in such matters! The market value of an ox, circa 1300, was 13s. 6d. (67.5p).

All but the very poorest of manorial households kept a few cows and these valuable animals provided milk, from which butter and cheese were produced; meat; and their hides were used to make leather. The quantity and quality of the milk yield declined between Michaelmas and the following spring due to the poor winter feeding. That part of the produce which was surplus to the needs of the villeins was sold or bartered. In 1300, a cow produced an average of 98 lbs. of cheese and 7 lbs. of butter between May and Michaelmas. A cow or bull had a market value of about 10s. (50p), and a cow could be rented out at between 5s. (25p) and 6s. (30p) for the season.

Also of great importance were the sheep which, although harder to manage than pigs and not so useful as the oxen, were considered to be almost a necessity. Their wool, skins and meat were of prime use and importance, as was their fertilizing function in the fields and meadows, and even their milk was used to eke out other supplies. Hence, even although the Lords of the Manor sometimes had rights over their fertilizing functions, they were of sufficient value to form part of almost every villein's stock.

It was the pigs, however, that ranked highest in the villein's estimation. No other animal was so easily fed, fattened, or so quickly ready for slaughter. The village swineherd was of great importance. It was he who gathered together the swine and drove them into the manorial woodland, at such times as they were thrown open to the villeins, to feed on the acorns.

At other times the swine were driven onto the wastelands and the fallow field to get what food they could find. Unless they could obtain the greatest portion of the pig feed in this way it was considered highly unprofitable to keep them. It was only in the very hardest months of winter that it was considered economically sound to supply the pigs with anything but waste and what they could get by rooting in the wastelands.

As well as the foregoing livestock vast flocks of all kinds of chickens and other poultry were kept. Most manorial records show that the peasants were obliged to give gifts of large quantities of eggs to the Lords of the Manor at certain times of the year. Geese were also fairly commonly kept sometimes in such numbers as to requite the appointment of a village gooseherd.

Hunting and Fishing

There were of course other sources of food which were available to the manorial peasants. In the woodlands and wastes wild life was abundant and the rivers and ponds teemed with fish. However, most Lords of the Manor enjoyed rights of 'free warren,' which had been granted by the Kings and overlords, which gave them and their nominees exclusive rights to hunt the 'beasts of the warren,' i.e. rabbits, foxes, hares and wild birds in the manorial woodlands.

It was the pigs, however, that ranked highest in the villein's estimation. No other animal was so easily fed, fattened, or so quickly ready for slaughter.

The King reserved exclusive rights to hunt in the Royal forests, which were enclosed against all others by the 'forest pale' or fence. Of course the King could not be prevented from chasing 'beasts of the forest' (e.g. deer or wild boar) over the manorial woodlands if they escaped beyond the 'forest pale.' Rights of 'free warren' therefore did not entitle the Lords of the Manor to enclose their woodlands.

Due to this inability to enclose their woodlands the Lords had great difficulty in enforcing their rights of 'free warren' against the peasants. Either from desperation of devilment, the peasants took whatever they wanted and poaching was widespread. If a peasant was unlucky enough to be caught he was dealt with in the Manorial Courts although they mostly got away with it.

As with hunting rights, the Lords of the Manor also tried to reserve fishing rights to themselves. All the great manor houses had their own fishponds within the demesne lands and throughout the year fresh and salt fish from pond, river and sea formed part of the diet of the upper classes. However, as with free warren, it was almost impossible for the Lord's officials to enforce fishing rights against the peasants, who again believed that God helped those who helped themselves!

Pigeons

One universal source of resentment was the nuisance caused by the Lords of the Manor's pigeons. These birds were kept to provide variety of diet at the Lord's table and were considered a great luxury. It was the exclusive right of the Lords of the Manor to keep pigeons and every manor house had its dovecot. Even though the pigeons descended in great hoards onto the villeins' fields and devoured their crops, they could not be killed or interfered with. The villeins had to stand helplessly by and watch these hungry pests grow fat on their corn, peas and beans in order to provide a delicate luxury for the Lords and their household. It is little wonder therefore that the dovecote became one of the most hated symbols of the Lord's domain over the villeins.

The foregoing short examination of the manorial serfs gives the impression that, given reasonable harvests, life was not too difficult for the 30 acre holder. However, these larger holders were not typical and most villeins held much less. From what is known of the medieval corn yields it can be said that a holding of at least 10 acres was required to grow the minimum crop required to sustain an average peasant family. Those villeins and 'undermanni' who held less than this were forced to seek ways of augmenting their incomes such as working on wealthier men's holdings; as servants in the manor house; as communal shepherds or swineherds; or at one of the various village trades.

Rents and Services
Due to the Lord of the Manor

Serf and freemen spent much of their time at similar labour but there was a great gulf between them in other ways. Once the freeman had paid his yearly rent not much else was required of him by his Lord except perhaps some trifling service. The serf found things much more oppressive. Not only did he pay his rent, but a number of other small cash payments were exacted.

For example, he had to pay a yearly 'wood-penny' to take wood from the wasteland; he had to give a hen or some eggs at set seasons for the privilege of keeping poultry; if he sold a beast the Lord received part of the sale price; he had to pay his Lord to allow his daughter to marry; he could not have his son educated without again putting his hand in his pocket; and at all times he found himself unable to do what his free neighbour could do.

The Custom of the Manor

The restrictions of the serf's life were many, and although most of them were petty some were more irksome and all were a constant reminder of his servile status. Over the centuries a state of affairs had developed between Lord and serf which became known as 'the custom of the manor.' In theory the will of the Lord was all compelling, thus it may be said that any privilege or relaxation of the letter of the law was a result of the Lord's indulgence. In practice they only 'allowed' what they were powerless to stop.

A strong steward or bailiff on the one hand, or a determined body of serfs on the other, could make vast changes on any one manor in a very short time, especially in the days before the 'custom of the manor' was written down and memory had to be relied on. For many decades after the conquest, change was continuous on all manors. A state of flux existed in which the Lords and serfs each struggled to obtain their own ends.

Sometimes the Lords were beneficent and at others the reverse. In either case they exercised great powers over the lives of their serfs. The 'custom of the manor' gradually evolved out of the proceedings of the Manorial Courts. It therefore can be said, with some truth, that these customs were determined by the serfs because it was they who gave the 'dooms,' (i.e. the formal judgements made in the Manorial Courts), which constituted these customs.

However, a powerful lord or a harsh steward could always obtain a favourable verdict in these courts by force, intimidation, or biased interpretation of precedent. By the mid-thirteenth century most Lords were using the written word to record the 'custom of the manor' at the time of its creation in the Manor Courts. Thereafter the speed at which customs changed slowed down. Henceforward the memory of the 'wiser and saner' peasants was no longer relied on in the Manor Courts to define the existing custom and any dispute relating thereto could be resolved by immediate reference to the written record which was always interpreted in the Lord's favour!

This led to continuous contention between the serfs and their Lords - the former seeking to improve their status and the latter to enforce and consolidate their feudal rights. When giving their 'dooms' in the Manor Courts the serfs were sworn to base their opinions on their knowledge of the facts and to give their verdicts according to practical judgement. Thus they did their best to interpret matters in their own favour as often as possible. However, the written records were compiled by trained lawyers acting under the stewards, who were also trained lawyers. The serfs were therefore more likely than otherwise to get a rough deal in the Manorial Courts whose procedures were mostly beyond their comprehension.

No general account of the above process is possible because of the great variations in conditions between manors, even where several manors were under one Lord. The serfs' fight for better conditions went on for several centuries and the rigid cash basis on which most manors were conducted encouraged them to purchase freedom from many of their obligations whenever they got the chance. The status of villein finally disappeared in the sixteenth century by which time the power of the feudal barons had long since disappeared.

'Week-Work' and 'Boon-Work'

There was one characteristic feature of the manorial system which above all others separated the serfs from the freemen. This symbol of servility was the serf's obligation to spend part of each week doing manual labour on his Lords demesne lands as part of the return he paid for the privilege of holding land on the manor - the 'week-work.' Most villeins paid various rents as well as their 'week-work' obligations, but the latter were all important. The Lords depended to a great extent on this labour for the cultivation of their demesne lands, the care of their livestock, and the upkeep of their manor houses.

Most Lords, it is true, employed a nucleus of full-time servants who lived on the demesne. As time passed they allowed increasing numbers of their serfs to commute all or some part of their week-work obligations by paying 'quit-rents' in lieu. Nevertheless, for a long time over a large part of England many thousands of villeins and other serfs were obliged to leave their own affairs for part of each week to work for their Lords.

The actual obligations demanded in any particular instance varied from manor to manor. In general the 'week-work' demanded depended on size - the larger the holding the more onerous were the obligations that attached to it.

However, no account was taken of the size of the holder's family. Thus the seemingly burdensome obligations of a 30 acre holding looked much less daunting if the holder had a large family and, perhaps, servants of his own. Such a villein was able to plough his own fields without hindrance and he performed his obligations to his Lord by sending one or more members of his family to the manor.

In practice it was rarely necessary for the Lords to demand the full quotas of 'week-work' from their serfs. For instance a typical obligation to perform one or two days work a week for the Lord, whatever the original intention may have been, was only demanded on a day to day basis according to the Lord's actual need.

However, a strict account was kept of the actual number of days worked by each serf. The balance of their obligatory work days were either 'sold' back to the serfs and commuted, or held in reserve to be demanded at times of extra need such as ploughing, haymaking and harvest times.

On most manors the definition of just what constituted an acceptable 'days work' was specified by 'custom of the manor.' Such accepted definitions were usually liberal enough to allow the serf some leeway to work at his own affairs for some part of an obligatory work day.

During the period between Lammas (1st August) and Michaelmas (29th September) the gathering of the Lord's hay and grain harvest was given absolute priority over all things including the serf's own harvest. During this time the demand on the serf's labour was at its highest and they were called upon to provide a number of 'boon-days' as well as extra 'week-work.'

These 'boon-days' were in theory freely given by the serfs out of love for their Lords, but this freedom (and no doubt the love!) was more theoretical than real. The 'boon-days' often required the presence of the villein's entire household on the demesne fields.

During the period between Lammas (1st Aug) and Michaelmas (29th Sept) the gathering of the Lord's hay and grain harvest was given absolute priority over all things including the serf's own harvest.

The 'week-works,' during the rest of the year, from Michaelmas to the following August, centred on ploughing, manuring, harrowing, sowing and assisting the skilled men in the upkeep of the manor house. The serfs could also be on call to provided carrying services, such as carting produce to the towns to be sold.

Such in brief were the various services demanded by the Lords under the English manorial system. There was of course great variation both in the services demanded and the severity with which they were enforced but, in general, they were an inseparable part of the villein's life and a constant reminder of his serfdom. Absences from 'week-work' through sickness, attendance at the Manorial or Sheriff Courts, or on holy-days was dealt with according to 'custom of the manor' as was the enforced suspension of work due to bad weather.

Military Service

The liability of the villeins to perform military service was only imposed on them gradually. Unlike their manorial services their military ones had nothing to do with their serfdom and were entirely due to the King's ever growing demands for manpower to fight his wars. Eventually the demand became so insistent that even the remotest peasants were shaken from their secluded lives and into an awareness of a much wider world.

The majority of English peasants lived very isolated lives. They rarely travelled more than twenty or so miles from their village beyond which, to them, was the great unknown of which they had no knowledge at first hand and not much more by repute! For about 150 years after the Conquest the peasants knew nothing of war although, in unusual emergencies, they could be summoned by the Sheriffs for local defence purposes known as the shire levy. These levies mostly consisted of ill-disciplined, untrained, and ill-led rabbles armed only with cudgels.

Assize of Arms

In 1181 King Henry II issued the first Assize of Arms which decreed that all citizens, burgesses and freeman who held land should arm themselves according to their means thus removing this duty from the feudal Barons. A writ of Henry III in 1225 extended the Assize of Arms to include any villeins who held lands above a certain value. A later writ in 1242 enlarged its scope still further to include all villeins regardless of the value of their holdings. It was with forces thus raised and armed that King Edward I attacked the Welsh in 1277.

Each man paid for his own equipment, the country bore the cost of mobilisation, and the crown paid wages from the date of the outward march. In 1277 it was the Sheriffs who mustered the shire forces and led them to war. However, as the years passed the King appointed special officers to take over these duties from the Sheriffs.

These officials were known as the Commissioners of Array and they were issued with writs authorizing them to raise specified numbers of men from the shires. The Commissioners were usually experienced officers and were often sent, war after war, to the same shires and, no doubt, they got to know the right men to choose.

Statute of Winchester

King Edward I found that the existing measures were inadequate to provide the numbers of men required by the growing importance of infantry in warfare. By the Statute of Winchester 1285, he recognized the entire military resources of the country and brought all peasants aged between 16 and 60, regardless of whether they held land or not, within the reach of the King's Commissioners of Array.

From that time onward the peasants were more and more liable to find themselves involved in one or other of the constant wars in France, Scotland or Wales the ultimate aims of which were probably completely beyond their comprehension.

At first it was mainly the peasants in the Welsh, and later Scotch, border counties who were forced to march at the King's command. In later times the continental wars necessitated the raising of suitable recruits from all over England. There is no reason to suppose that there was any great enthusiasm for such adventures amongst the peasants. They were untrained in war, and slow to see any great advantage to be gained by leaving their fields to fight in an unknown land. Such travellers' tales as they heard of the wild and barbaric Scots and Welsh did little to allay their antipathy.

It can therefore be said with reasonable certainty that the King's Commissioners were hard pressed to raise the numbers of men required. Although the King paid them twopence or threepence a day (as compared to a penny a day which was the going day rate for field work), and although they were seldom kept on active service for more than three months at a time, the fear of the unknown and reluctance to leave home kept most men from volunteering. However, the Commissioners had to find the men somehow and it was almost always necessary to resort to compulsion.

The peasants were more and more liable to find themselves involved in one or other of the constant wars in France, Scotland or Wales, the ultimate aims of which were probably completely beyond their comprehension!

Muster Rolls

The Commissioners were assisted in their task by the Muster Rolls that were compiled in each shire hundred by the local constables. From these rolls they were able to see the names of all those available for service in each village and how they were armed - e.g. long bow, knife, cudgel, pike or halberd (a combined spear and battle-axe). Thus the Commissioners were able to select men of the right categories in sufficient numbers to comply with the Royal writs.

The King instructed the Commissioners to explain his objects and war aims to the peasant recruits in a reasonable, patient and courteous manner. The King also authorised the payment of various gratuities, additional to their normal pay, to induce them to march willingly. However, as well as these fair words he decreed that the Commissioners should bring to justice and punish those peasants who rebelled or disobeyed orders. Although the Commissioners may have succeeded in making the peasants march, they found that making them fight, or even stay in the battle zone, was another matter and many took the first opportunity to desert.

Medieval records have survived which show that desertion was commonplace. An analysis of the pay-roll of King Edward I's Scottish campaign of 1300 shows that although 16,000 men were ordered to be at Carlisle on 24th June only 3,500 had arrived by 1st July, and the most the Commissioners could muster by mid-July was 7,600 men. That was the peak strength achieved, and the force gradually drained away thereafter, until in August only 3,000 men remained! Some, no doubt, had been killed or wounded and others had served their full time and been honourably discharged but the majority of these peasant soldiers had deserted and trudged back to their more peaceful fields. It is easy to imagine these returned conscripts entertaining their fellow serfs in the village ale-houses with exaggerated tales of their adventures in the manner of all such reluctant 'heroes' through the ages.

During the fourteenth century even heavier demands for military service were made on serfs, and the effects were felt in every village of the land. But even though the bowmen and infantry, who won such famous battles as Crecy in 1346, had trained on the village greens of England, there is no reason to suppose that military service was any more popular with the serfs than it had been in earlier times. Recruiting methods became even more coercive and, whereas the better off could often bribe officials and get out of serving, the serfs had nothing to offer and found themselves inducted into the forces while the richer faint-hearts who could grease palms got off. Thus the serfs, as in many other situations, had to suffer in silence because they knew of nobody who was powerful or learned enough to voice their grievances.

Other Servile Burdens

Even after the villeins had paid their rents, performed their 'week-work' and given their 'boon-days,' they were still under many other obligations to the Lords of the Manors. Their lack of freedom showed in many ways; they could not grind their own corn, bake their own bread, sell their own animals, nor do many other things without their Lord's permission. They were constantly reminded of the Lord's power and they lived in fear of the visits of the stewards and bailiffs, whose authoritative commands had to be respected. They were also under the supervision of the village officials - the reeve, the beadle, the hayward, etc. The following is a brief outline of some of these additional burdens and it leaves no room for wonder that the serfs so passionately and consistently sought to buy their freedom.

The Manorial Mill

Every Lord of the Manor owned one or more mills where all kinds of grain could be ground, Sometimes the Lords employed their own millers and sometimes they leased the mills out at a yearly rent based on the amount of corn ground. In both cases the Lords insisted that their serfs had their corn ground exclusively at the manorial mill at the Lord's own price.

The mill was therefore a valuable source of the Lord's income and was often referred to as a separate item when the value of a manor was being assessed. In view of this value the Lords took great trouble to see that their mills had ample business and that the profit therefrom was not threatened by competition. This they achieved by their insistence that the unfree must bring their corn to the manorial mill to be ground. Failure to do so resulted in fines being imposed on offenders at the Manorial Court.

The millers' monopoly, and the lack of competition it caused, resulted in a very inefficient service. Regardless of the demands of manorial custom men were always trying to avoid their 'suit of mill' either by seeking better service from the Lord's competitors or else covertly grinding their own corn at home, using small hand mills called 'querns.' If caught in these activities the serfs were fined and their querns were confiscated.

In some very rare circumstances, Lords granted licences which permitted the holders to have their corn ground wherever they pleased. This privilege, of course, was never freely given. In most cases when a serf was caught in the act of taking corn to a rival mill custom decreed that the Lord was entitled to seize the offender's horse and the Lord's miller was entitled to confiscate whatever corn or flour the offender had on him at the time he was apprehended.

The millers collected the grinding fees, or 'multures,' at the mill as soon as the corn was delivered to them, Every serf or freeman who used the mill, except the parish priest, had to pay a multure which usually consisted of a pre-set portion of their total grain. In the thirteenth century the average multure paid by freemen was 1/24th of their grain and serfs had to contribute 1/16th of theirs. However, the price of grain, and the multure charged, varied considerably from year to year and the poorer the harvest the greater was the multure demanded.

It is not surprising that the millers acquired a reputation for dishonesty. 'What is the boldest thing in the world?' asks a medieval riddle; the answer 'A miller's shirt, because it clasps a thief by the throat every day!' Some of the sharp practice of the millers can be seen in the old court records which show they watered grain to increase its weight; changed the corn entrusted to them and gave 'worse for better;' they fed their hogs and chickens on the grain in their keeping; and fattened their 'gluttonous geese' by the same means! Chaucer's miller in 'The Canterbury Tales' is typical.

The two factors which probably caused the most friction and bad blood were firstly, that the parish priests, regardless of their comparative wealth, were exempt from paying multure. Secondly, the serfs who were compelled to use the Lord's mills were charged 1/16th of their corn for multure. Freemen, on the other hand, were only charged 1/24th of theirs, and could get it ground wherever they pleased.

The Manorial Oven and Bakery

Just as the serfs could not grind their corn wherever they pleased, so they were forbidden to bake bread at home or anywhere other than in the Lord's oven. Most serfs, it is true, could not have baked at home even if they were skilled enough to build an oven as they could not have used it in their flimsy houses without grave risk to themselves and their neighbours. Therefore, providing the Lord or his tenant baker did not overcharge the serfs, the village oven or bakehouse was more of a communal convenience that a manorial oppression.

The oven provided income for the Lord, often at no trouble to himself, because he usually let it out at a rent either to a skilled baker or to all his serfs on a communal basis. There are many records of serfs being fined for not baking at the manorial oven.

Both the mill and the oven were common sights on the medieval manors. What rendered these monopolies so odious was not so much the fixed tariffs or the prohibitions against crushing your own grain and baking bread at home. The most irksome aspects were the compulsion to carry the corn for great distance, over abominable roads, and then perhaps having to wait two or three days at the door of the mill because the mill-pool had run dry or the miller had more work that he could cope with.

Further aggravation was caused by often having to accept poorly ground meal, burned or half-baked bread, and enduring all sorts of sharp practices by the millers and bakers.

Tallage

As well as paying rent, as did his free neighbours, the serfs were also forced to make various other payments from time to time to meet the diverse needs of their Lords. These payments were a form of tax and were often demanded at times of great stress, when the serfs were least able to meet them. The most onerous of these burdens were tallage, heriot and mortuary. Tallage was a form of tax which was levied by the Lords of the Manors on their unfree tenants.

During the hundred years or so that followed the Norman Conquest, tallage was demanded by the Lords in a completely arbitrary manner. So far as the purpose, the amount, or the frequency of the demands was concerned the serfs had no redress. Thus 'tallage at will,' not unreasonably, came to be regarded by the lawyers as one of the main tokens of serfdom. Certainly the right of one man to exact from another for any purpose he desired, any sum he thought fit, at uncertain intervals, came very close to complete subjection. This practice was justified by the medieval legal theory that everything a serf possessed belonged to his Lord.

The serf generally strove to obtain some certainty in these matters. From the twelfth century onwards the Lord's rights to demand 'tallage at will' gradually became modified and fixed by custom of the manors. Little by little thereafter 'tallage at will' was replaced by 'fixed tallage,' i.e. the demands were made for yearly amounts fixed by general consent in the Manorial Courts.

This state of affairs was only won after much effort by the serfs in the Medieval Courts. 'Fixed tallage' removed the uncertainty, which was the worst feature of 'tallage at will,' and once achieved it became easier for the serf to buy himself free of the service taint of tallage by paying the Lord to allow him to include it in his yearly rent. However, as long as a peasant was subject to tallage, whether 'fixed' or 'at will,' the law would declare him to be an unfree serf, regardless of how rich or free of other servile burdens he may have been.

The right of one man to exact from another for any purpose he desired, any sum he thought fit, at uncertain intervals, came very close to complete subjection. It was justified by the theory that everything a serf possessed belonged to his Lord.

A legal opinion concerning a Lord's right to impose new tallages given in 1285 by Richard de Masia Villa, a medieval English legal expert, sums up the position thus "... the subjects are either serfs or freemen. If they be serfs they are bound to pay the tallages newly imposed on them, even though they tend to profit the Lord alone; for serfs and their possessions are the property of their Lords. In the case of freemen, if those tallages be in no way to the profit of the community, then neither King nor prince can impose such tallages on his free subjects. The reason here is that the possessions of free subjects are not the property of their Lords."

The distinction that was made in the above opinion between tallage imposed for the Lord's personal gain and for communal purposes is of interest. It seems to imply that the common law would have upheld the Lord's right to impose tallage on their free tenants, providing it was exacted for some kind of communal benefit. In the latter case, tallage could be said to have been a rudimentary form of local taxation.

Heriots

Even when a serf died his Lord made claim on his possessions known as 'heriots.' The church also made similar claims on a dead serf's property, known as a 'mortuary' which is described in the chapter on the Church and the Manor. The concept of the 'heriot' arose out of an old custom whereby all men, free or bond, were bound to arrange for the return, after their death, of the 'hergeat,' or war gear, which their Lord had originally issued to them. In later centuries when it became the legal duty of all freemen to provide their own personal arms. the Lords no longer had grounds to claim 'heriot' from them, and therefore their obligation lapsed.

The serfs were not so fortunate. Since they were obliged from time to time to give military service, and since all they possessed legally belonged to their Lords, it was held that serfs received their weapons from their Lords. Therefore, on a serf's death, his heirs had to pay a 'heriot' which usually took the form of either his best beast or his most valuable chattel. Three ancient legal theories were present in the 'heriots' that were imposed in the later middle ages:

❑ That when a warrior died his heirs must return his arms to the Lord who had issued them

❑ The heirs of a peasant, who had received his original farm stock and equipment from his Lord, must recognize the Lord's ownership of that stock by yielding to him the best beast or article.

❑ All the possessions of a serf legally belonged to his Lord and therefore after the serf's death the Lord took the best of them to proclaim his ownership.

Thus, even after death the poor serf still had to pay his dues to the Lord of the Manor.

Manorial Administration

$\mathfrak{F}$rom the foregoing description of the medieval manors it is obvious that the Lords required considerable organizing ability to control their peasants and fully exploit their demesne lands. In those, quite rare, instances where the Lords resided in the manor house and supervised their own workers, it was a comparatively easy task. With a small number of appointed officials, they could collect the rents, fines, boons and tallages and ensure that the services due from the villeins and other serfs were effectively rendered.

For many Lords life was not so simple. They often held more than one manor and these could be scattered over a whole shire, or perhaps over half of England! Even without other affairs to concern them, it would have been impossible for such Lords to have overseen their manors efficiently. In many cases they were busy servants of the King, perhaps great soldiers engaged in foreign wars and crusades, or followers of the Royal Court who despised the country life except perhaps for the hunting it provided! The great ecclesiastical landowners, such as Bishops, Abbots and Abbesses, were also unable to personally supervise their manors.

Extents and Customals

Hence a widespread system developed whereby the manors were controlled by paid agents of the Lords and a whole hierarchy of officials and minor servants were created. The Lords gave their chief officials, the stewards, the clearest account possible of what lands and people they had to control, and what they could expect from the manorial population by way of money, kind and services. The two classes of documents which provided this information were the 'extents' and the 'customals.'

The 'extents' set out in meticulous detail exactly what was to be demanded by way of rents and services from every tenant on the manor, whether freeman or serf. The 'customals' were written records of the by-laws necessitated by changes over the years to the 'customs of the manor.' Most of what is known of the administration of the medieval manors comes from surviving 'extents' and 'customals,' together with the records of the Manor Courts.

Handbooks on Estate Management

Several handbooks on estate management, which were mostly written in the late thirteenth century, have also survived. An example of the latter is 'Walter of Henley,' edited by E. Lamond in 1890 and published by the Royal Historical Society.

These handbooks tend to give somewhat idealised descriptions of manorial administration. The duties of the various manorial officials, as defined therein, are not universally confirmed in the 'customals' or Court Rolls. In fact, the latter often gives the impression that the scribes who compiled them, and the contemporary lawyers, could not differentiate very clearly between the various manorial officers.

No doubt on some of the larger manors there was a hierarchy of officials and servants such as is described in 'Walter of Henley.' However, on many smaller manors a more primitive organisation existed in which fewer officials each performed several functions. In practice, very wide variations of procedure and customs existed, even between manors only a few miles apart.

To consider the manorial organisation it is necessary to study the needs of the greater Lords, such as the Bishops or great nobles, to run their estates, which often consisted of several manors. The personnel involved can be divided into two main groups, the administrators and the servants - the latter being the select band of manual workers who were vital to the running of the manor house and the proper cultivation of the demesne lands. The highest ranks of administrators were all freemen, while those in the lower ranks, as well as the manual workers, were drawn from the Lord's serfs.

The Steward

The steward was the highest ranking of the manorial officials and was authorised to act as his Lord's agent in all matters pertaining to the running of the manorial estates. On taking office he was sworn on oath to preserve his Lord's interests to the utmost of his abilities.

His importance may be judged by comparing his salary with that of the other officials. For example, in 1300 a typical steward's salary was £15 a year, plus extra payments for dealing with the King's writs. His fur trimmed robes of office were paid for by his Lord and he received an allowance of hay, litter and firewood from each manor in the estate. On the other hand, the bailiff received £6 per annum, still a goodly sum in those days, while at the lower end a reeve got a mere 9s. (45p) per annum.

The steward's duties were wide and varied. He appointed the lesser officials; he was responsible for all matters concerning the management and agricultural exploitation of the manors; he presided over the Manor Courts and held 'View of Frankpledge' (see later chapter on the Manorial Courts). Thus he needed first and foremost a thorough knowledge of the laws and customs of the various manors which comprised the Lord's estates.

He also needed to know the size of each of the Lord's manors and how many acres should be ploughed and what quantity of seed would be required. He had to know all his bailiffs and reeves and how well they conducted the Lord's business and how they treated the serfs.

He needed to know how many halfpenny loaves could be made from a quarter of corn and how many cattle each pasture would support. He had to be ever watchful that none of his Lord's rights lapsed or were usurped, and that none of his lands were encroached upon. He had to think always of his Lord's needs, both in terms of money and produce, and to see that they were constantly supplied.

After Michaelmas each year, the steward summoned before him all those underlings he had charged with the day to day running of the manors. From them he extracted a detailed account of their activities and enquired into the use made of every animal and the produce resulting therefrom down to the very last egg! The exact results of the years harvest were enquired into and recorded and the amounts received from the tenants in rents, fines, and in every other way, had to be accounted for. This examination was so searchingly conducted that it must have terrified the humble rustics to such an extent that they were too intimidated to try and cheat.

President of the Manor Courts

The most important of the many functions which the Lords entrusted to their stewards was that of president of the Manor Courts. These were held at regular intervals on every manor on the Lords' estates and the steward, as the Lord's deputy, was the sole dispenser of justice therein.

It is easy to imagine how important the steward must have seemed to the simple peasants as he rode up to the manor house on the eve of the Manor Court, probably escorted by his men-at-arms. His retinue of servants would have followed him at a respectful distance, and with him would have ridden his clerk who carried the precious Court Rolls in his saddle-bag. The Rolls usually contained many things the peasants would sooner have forgotten. To them the clerk and his master the steward must have seemed to have had every detail of their lives and misdemeanours at their fingertips.

In reality the stewards were very unapproachable and the only personal contact the average villein ever had with them was in the Manor Courts. Much closer to the peasant, often in daily contact, were the various lesser officials. The two most important of these were the bailiff and the reeve.

It is easy to imagine how important the steward must have seemed to the simple peasants as he rode up to the manor house on the eve of the Manor Court, probably escorted by his men-at-arms.

The Bailiff

The extent to which bailiffs and reeves were employed on the manors varied greatly as there were many different systems and manorial customs. Sometimes both a bailiff and a reeve were active on one manor and sometimes a bailiff was in charge of several manors and travelled between them to supervise their effective working. Smaller estates, e.g. those consisting of only one manor, often had no bailiff at all and were supervised by a reeve acting directly under the steward. Those bailiffs who had charge of several manors were paid extra and given the title of sergeant, but their basic duties were the same as those of the ordinary bailiffs.

Whatever title they were given the sergeants or bailiffs stood apart from the other dwellers on the manors, Not only were they freemen, they also enjoyed the prestige which came from their position as their Lord's mouthpiece. They were usually supplied by the Lord, or his steward acting on his behalf, with a charter of authority which provided identity and set out their duties in detail. Some such formal authorisation was very necessary because there are a number of cases on record of men fraudulently purporting to be bailiffs for their own financial gains.

The official status of the bailiffs was proclaimed before the steward at the first Manor Court to be held after any new appointment. At this time the new bailiff took the oath of fealty, swearing to 'behave honestly toward the county, towards rich and poor,' and to guard the Lord's rights. Their high rank was further emphasised by the fact that they dwelt in the manor house, at their Lord's expense, in special quarters reserved for them. From these apartments they superintended the running of the whole manor and also kept a close watch on the activities of the full-time manorial servants who lived in out-buildings close to the manor house.

The Bailiffs' Duties

The bailiffs' duties were many. They put into effect the agricultural policy which had been decided on in consultation with the stewards and set the tasks to be performed; directing labour accordingly. They had full discretion to decide how the 'day-work' obligations of the serfs might best be used and they dealt with the day to day problems which arose on every field on the manors. They also ensured that the serfs paid their rents and tallages and that the manorial obligations were performed effectively and in full. They had to know the limits of what could be demanded, as laid down in the 'extents' and 'customals,' but within these limits their powers were extensive.

With such sweeping powers there was bound to be some corruption and the bailiffs were often unpopular with the manorial population. Among the recorded malpractices of the unscrupulous bailiffs are compelling the serfs to buy ale from them at twice the legal price; extorting illegitimate carrying and harvest services; disregarding the 'custom of the manor' themselves; and taking bribes to disregard similar breaches by others. Of course the bailiffs were well aware that the coming of the stewards gave an opportunity for the peasants to seek redress of their wrongs in the Manor Court and there was always the danger that the steward himself would notice the irregularities.

By and large the bailiffs escaped serious criticism in the Manor Courts as their status was so far above the serfs, and they always had the ear of the stewards who generally took their sides. However, soon after Michaelmas each year the bailiffs had to face the Lord's auditors who were not so easy to hoodwink! They had to give details of how their Lord's money had been spent and to what profit. If a bailiff was unable to satisfy the auditors he was liable to be surcharged.

The Reeve

On all manors, whether they were large or small, there was one official whose presence was universal, namely the reeve. This officer was always chosen from amongst the serfs - freemen were exempt from service as reeves. The reason for this was that proof of past service as a reeve, or even of a liability so to serve, was accepted in the King's Courts as legal proof of a man's servile status. For his lowly origins, the reeve was of great importance to the efficient running of the manors. Unlike the bailiff, who was imposed on the peasants from outside, the reeve was himself a peasant. He had known every field of the manor since his boyhood and was acquainted with the habits of every serf who lived in his village.

It is reasonable to suppose that the reeves were often more effective in the day to day running of the manors than the 'outsider' bailiffs. This contention is further supported by the fact that the manorial records show it was the reeves, just as often as the bailiffs, who presented the manorial accounts to the Lord's auditors. The fact that a serf was ever trusted to this extent suggests that the reeves were not so insignificant as their low remuneration and servile status seems to indicate. Service as a reeve was extremely onerous and far from universally popular. Given the opportunity many peasants avoided performing the service altogether.

By and large the bailiffs escaped serious criticism in the Manor Courts as their status was so far above the serfs, and they always had the ear of the stewards who generally took their sides.

The Lord's saw the reeves and their detailed knowledge of the manors and customs, as well as their permanent presence thereon, as an assurance that on every manor there was one man who could be held strictly accountable for all aspects of the manorial economy for 365 days a year - and cheaply too! The Lords therefore saw it as essential to their interests to enforce this service from the villeins.

In practice it was only the 'virgaters' (villeins holding 30 or more acres) who were chosen to serve as reeves. Villeins with 15 acres were selected to serve as beadles, constables, haywards or tithingmen, but the remainder of the unfree tenants were rarely called on to be officials of any kind. Of course the reason for this was that many of the villeins who held 30 acres or more employed the poorer serfs on their holdings and the latter would have had a hard time if set over the 'virgaters' who employed them.

Selection of the Reeve

The reeves were chosen either by selection by the Lord; preliminary selection of two or three candidates by the peasants and final selection by the Lord; or outright democratic election by the peasants. The most ancient of these methods was autocratic selection but the general trend was towards democratic election by the peasants; this at least gave the illusion that the peasants had some control over their own affairs. Once chosen, by whatever method, the reeve was immediately sworn in by the Lord or steward in the presence of the assembled Manor Court - hence there could be no doubt who the reeve was.

A reeves' term of office was, in theory, for one year. However, if they showed aptitude for their work the Lords were only too willing to continue their appointments from year to year, and records of reeves serving for twenty or more years are common. We can therefore assume that at least some of the reeves served willingly and possibly even took great pride in their office.

Gradually, by purchase or other means, more villeins obtained the right to elect their own reeves. However, once this privilege had been won the serfs often found themselves at a disadvantage. Most Lords contended that those who held their land in villeinage, if privileged to elect their own reeves, were collectively responsible for the efficiency of those they elected. Thus the peasants could be forced to compensate their Lords for any losses incurred by them due to the incompetence of their chosen reeves.

Once provision for the democratic election of the reeves had been written into the customals, many peasants purchased exemption from election. The willingness of the peasants to pay these, often quite considerable, sums is an indication of the onerous nature of the reeveship. No doubt these purchased exemptions explain the fact that on some manors the reeveship devolved solely on the holders of certain lands.

The Reeves' Duties

The reeves were involved in virtually every aspect of the manorial economy. Among other things, they had to see that the farm workers rose early and got to work quickly; they oversaw the ploughing, carting, manuring, seeding and harvesting; they kept a close watch on the serfs to ensure there was neither waste or theft; and they supervised the livestock and saw to their well-being. It was their duty to issue food allowances to the servants, and they also had to bring before the Manor Court all those who failed in their service obligations. The reeve was also responsible for the upkeep of the manor house, farm buildings and all the agricultural implements belonging to the manor.

Sometimes the reeves' duties took them far away from their manors in pursuit of their Lord's interests. Some travelled large distances to markets to buy and sell on their Lord's behalf. From time to time the reeves were called upon to attend the Hundred Court, with four of their fellow villeins, and there to answer for all things concerning their manors. Also twice yearly they had to appear before the King's itinerant justices at the Shire Courts. Thus the reeves were the chiefs of the peasants and were made full use of by their Lords.

The power entrusted to the reeves was often great, and they were frequently left in sole charge of the manorial labourers for weeks at a time. No doubt many were honest, but it is only natural that there were some who were corrupted by their powers and either deceived and swindled their Lords or oppressed their fellow villeins. Given the circumstances it would also be difficult to imagine that bribery did not exist or that favouritism did not flourish on many manors.

Of course if a reeve went too far his victim was entitled to make complaint and seek redress in the Manor Court. It was then up to the Lord or his steward to enquire into the matter and to determine the truth, usually by means of a manorial jury. Thus the reeves were limited in their powers to oppress their fellow villeins, always assuming the Lord was determined to see justice done and that the jurors were not too intimidated to speak their minds.

It is only natural that there were some who were corrupted by their powers and either deceived and swindled their Lords or oppressed their fellow villeins.

Generally speaking it was not so much the peasants as the Lords who were the victims of dishonest reeves! Given their opportunities, it is not too surprising that those reeves so inclined found ways to deceive their Lords, sometimes they even managed to fool the Lords' auditors, which was a much more difficult thing to do.

The Reeves' Wages

The task of the reeves was burdensome and it was not much relished by most of the villeins. There were, of course, emoluments and allowances which went with the appointment and in some part compensated for the onerous nature of the work. In most cases the reeves were given a salary, small when compared to the stewards and bailiffs, but at least double that of other peasants, such as a ploughman and herdsman.

On the vast majority of manors the reeves' salaries were paid entirely by the Lords. Variations of the latter method were customary on a few manors whereby the villeins were required to pay a levy, in addition to their annual rent, in order to pay the reeves' wages. The reeves' salaries were not the most important element of their total rewards as there were three other sources of benefit, namely the remission of rents, relaxation of their customary manorial obligations, and grants of extra meadow or closes.

The value of the first of these sources of reward is self evident and most reeves were excused the whole, or some part, of their annual rent during the term of their office. The relaxation of their customary manorial obligations was no doubt a great relief to the reeves. In practice it would have been almost impossible for anybody to have acted in the position and to have performed the customary 'week-work' obligation at the same time. Most Lords recognised this fact and fully released their reeves from such duties. However, there were some oppressive Lords who made their reeves pay fines in lieu of the 'week-work' the Lord's own demands had made them miss. Other Lords refused to relax any of the reeves' 'week-work' obligations except at harvest time.

Temporary grants of pieces of meadow or special closes provided valuable extra grazing rights for the reeves and were probably the most prized perquisites of their term of office. On some manors the latter perquisites took the form of rights to graze their cattle on the Lords' demesne meadow. In other places, the reeves were given an allowance of animal feed or certain 'closes' were set apart for the sole purpose of providing extra grazing for the reeves' animals. As an additional reward the reeves were sometimes given a share of the crops produced on the Lord's demesne.

On some manors the reeves were so much a part of the Lord's household that they could demand to eat their food daily with the Lord's other servants at the manor house, sometimes even at the Lord's table. On the majority of manors such rights to sustenance at the Lord's expense were confined to the harvest season.

At that busy time it was essential that the reeves were constantly at the head of agricultural activities in the manors. The Lords were therefore content to allow the reeves to feed with the other manorial servants during the harvest period - Lammas (1st August) to Michaelmas (29th September).

Some customals defined the period of the reeves' entitlement to this provision of sustenance as being the full period of Lammas to Michaelmas, others reduced it to only five weeks. Most customals emphasize the temporary nature of the arrangement by ending the relevant entry with some such words as '... and afterwards at this own table throughout the year.'

Thus the election, conditions of service, and rewards of the reeves varied according to the 'customs of the manor.' No Lord could extract from his reeve more than custom had determined proper nor could he withhold the customary rewards.

The reeves were very valuable servants, and a good reeve was a treasure not lightly to be neglected by his Lord. Hence certain reeves remained in office year after year and, if they were willing and fair, it was to everyone's advantage that they did so.

The reeves were very valuable servants, and a good reeve was a treasure not lightly to be neglected by his Lord.

The Hayward and Beadle

There were a number of other lesser manorial officers the unfree could be called upon to perform, the chief of these were those of the haywards and beadles. However, such manuals of manorial management as 'Walter of Henley' do not seem to classify these offices as being separate functions. In fact, these two services are so often found to be performed by one and the same person that any attempt at rigid demarcation of their duties tends to be somewhat academic.

For convenience it can be said that the haywards were basically in charge of all matters to do with the meadows and pastures. They impounded all animals that strayed into the meadows during the closed season - i.e. Christmas to Lammas; they kept watch on the pastures; maintained the fences; charged those who infringed the customary rights thereof; and they oversaw the hay-making.

At harvest times they assisted the reeves and supervised the peasants in the fields; they measured the sheaves of corn to ensure that they were the right size and stayed on the manor overnight to guard the Lord's corn against theft. At the end of the year the haywards produced a tally to the reeve of all those matters for which they had been made responsible.

The beadles, on the other hand, were basically the village policemen. Their duties were mostly associated with the functions of the Manorial Courts; they gave notice of all court sessions and summoned the peasants to attend them; they collected the fines that were imposed by the Courts and executed evictions when so ordered. They warned the peasants of their 'week-work' obligations and ensured that they reported to the demesne fields at the appropriate times. They also seized and impounded stray animals pending the Lord's will regarding them.

The haywards and/or beadles, like the reeves, were either elected or selected to serve according to local custom. It is probable that all three of these appointments developed in much the same way. Their remuneration and rewards were also similar, i.e. remission or partial remission of rents together with requisites and allowances and they also fed, at the Lord's expense, with the manorial servants during harvest time.

The scope of the haywards' and/or beadles' activities varied from manor to manor according to custom and need. However, unlike the reeves, they were not universally appointed. On the largest manors both a hayward and a beadle were often appointed; on the majority of manors both offices, if indeed they existed, were performed by one man; while on many of the smallest manors only a beadle was appointed as a servant of the Manor Court. In general the duties involved in these offices were never considered to be anything like as onerous as those of the ubiquitous reeves. Thus it was the villeins with the maximum sized holdings of fifteen or so acres that were elected or selected to perform them.

Woodwards and Foresters

Various other minor appointments were made to suit local needs, i.e. the woodwards, who safeguarded the Lord's woodlands and plantations and the foresters, who watched over the Lord's hunting rights. In certain areas, such as the fenlands and the coast, officers were appointed to inspect and report on the protecting dykes and sea defences. All these officers received similar rewards and privileges to the haywards.

The Manorial Accounts

The yearly accounts were usually returned by the reeves and their compilation probably caused them more trouble that the rest of their duties put together! These accounts were formidable and showed in the minutest detail every item of manorial income and expenditure.

It is hard to understand how the illiterate reeves managed to have such details available. The answer seems to have been that they relied on various tallies and notches on barn-posts etc., together, presumably, with excellent memories.

It is fairly certain that the highly detailed accounts that were produced in those days would have been utterly beyond the understanding of the average unlettered reeve. These written accounts were compiled from the data supplied by the reeves by specially trained scribes who made a yearly round of the manors, after Michaelmas, for this purpose. Indeed, one of the most common items in the accounts is the scribes fee for his services, together with the cost of the parchment used.

Where a Lord only had a small estate, the written accounts were often prepared by the priest, and many Bishops warned their clergy to avoid such worldly matters. It is not surprising that the priests were asked to perform this task in the absence of professional scribes as they were usually the only learned men in the village. In general the accounts followed a set form and those which survived strongly resemble each other regardless if which part of the realm they come from.

The accounts normally start by naming the manor, the year of the King's reign, and the official who presents the information, followed by the main items. First the arrears from the previous year; then the rents of all kinds; the sales of corn and stock; the perquisites of the court, fines, tallages, heriots, etc. Then came details of expenditure after which a balance is struck. On the back of the document the scribe entered an account of the produce of the manor and how it had been consumed together with a detailed inventory of the livestock.

The Auditor

The reeve was not finished with the accounts when the scribe had completed his task as the dreaded auditors still had to be faced! The auditors visited each manor and made a searching inquiry into the accounts. 'Walter of Henley' advises that the Lord should '... ordain that the accounts be heard every year, but not in one place but on all the manors separately, for thus can one quickly know everything, and understand the profit and loss ... and then can the auditors take inquest of the doings which are doubtful.'

The auditors visited each manor and made a searching inquiry into the accounts.

The latter manual also has much to say about the qualities and duties of a good auditor. He has to be '... a faithful and prudent man, well versed in his profession, and knowing all the points and details of the accounts and the rents, outlays, returns, stock etc. which they must contain. He must gear the plaints and wrongs of everybody who complains of the Lord's officers and make enquiry into all doubtful matters, and fine those who have been careless with the Lord's property.'

In general the auditors were men of considerable status. Their office and authority was legally recognised under the second Statute of Westminster 1285. When making their inquests they had at their disposal the account rolls for the previous years, and sometimes even the 'customals' and 'extents.' The simple reeves must have thought them possessed of seemingly uncanny knowledge of the manorial past when they checked the current accounts by reference to previous years figures.

Every item of the account was closely scrutinized and the reeves were minutely cross-questioned about any item which seemed unusual. If reeves made cash payments on the authority of his superiors, acceptable evidence of such authority had to be produced to the auditors otherwise the reeve could be charged with the amount involved as a debt. When the accounts had been fully checked and all 'forgotten' items added in and any expenses they considered excessive had been reduced, the auditors struck a final balance and the years profit or loss was revealed.

If there was a profit the reeve was expected to produce it there and then, but if a loss had been made it was an unpleasant matter for himself and his fellow villeins who could expect increased demands and tighter conditions in the following year! However, in most cases there was a profit and the reeve was held strictly accountable for it. The auditors held discretionary powers and would at times forgive a discrepancy of the 'weakness and poverty' of the reeve.

Often the reeves were not so fortunate and found themselves firmly saddled with repayment of any such shortages in the accounts as personal debts which became the first item of arrears to be shown on the next years accounts! Sometimes the Lords took a surety from the reeve to secure repayment of the debt, at other times the hapless reeve would find himself in the village stocks for 'arrears of his accounts' or even handed over to the Sheriff to be kept in the county gaol.

After the completion of the audit the auditor gave the reeve a document which discharged him from his office. This stated his debts to the Lord, if any, and set out what grain and stock was left on the manor. A duplicate document was sewn into the accounts for future reference. Once the reeve possessed this document of acquittal he could, if not reappointed, retire into the humble obscurity from which he had come.

The Manorial Courts

Attendance at the Manor Court was compulsory for all manorial tenants and the list of services owed by them to their Lords usually concluded with such words as '... and he owes suit of court from three weeks to three weeks.' This duty was one of the more irksome of the serfs' obligations as it kept them from cultivating their fields and closes and they rarely, if ever, fully understood its proceedings! The Manor Court, as its name implies, was held by the Lord of the Manor or his steward. Its origins were probably more ancient than the feudal system to which it was adapted after the Norman Conquest.

The powers assumed by these courts varies greatly. On some manors they dealt solely with the villeins and confined their activities to matters of manorial administration. On others manors both villeins and freeman were dealt with, and criminal as well as administrative matters occupied their attentions, often including breaches of the King's Peace which were more properly the domain of the King's Justices.

Both the Kings and their Lords were well aware of the truth of the proverb - 'Justice is great profit' - and constant efforts were made by the King's lawyers to limit the jurisdiction of the Manor courts, if only to swell the Royal income from the common law courts.

Edward I's 'Quo Warranto' commissioners, who he appointed under the Statute of Gloucester in 1278, made an exhaustive investigation into the powers being exercised by the Lords of the Manors and by what authority (i.e. 'quo warranto') they did so. They found that everywhere the Lords were exercising rights to which they had no claim whatsoever except 'ancient seisin' - i.e. long standing custom! By means of such assumed powers the Lords, in their Manorial Courts, had usurped many powers which the lawyers said belonged only to the King together with the profits therefrom.

Infangenethef and Outfangenethef

Some Lords were able to produce Royal Charters which seemed to grant them considerable 'sake and soke' - i.e. powers of local jurisdiction. Such charters usually granted 'toll and team' - i.e. rights to impose tolls and tallages, and rights to recover stolen goods and hang thieves.

The latter rights were of two kinds, 'infangenethef' - limited to the rights to those who were apprehended within the manors, and 'outfangenethef' - much less frequently encountered, that extended the right to enable a thief to be pursued outside the manor and brought back for trial and hanging.

The terms of these charters were usually so vague and uncertain that by the end of the thirteenth century the prevailing legal doctrine was that such terms were meaningless. Wise Lords took good care to obtain Royal Charters which were drafted in more exact language because the lawyers were objecting more and more to the vagueness of the old terminology and asking for powers that were granted in unclear terms to be extinguished. From 1287 onwards it became the practice for Royal Charters either to '... except those things which belong to the King's Crown,' or to '... except murder, treasure trove, rape, and breach of the peace.'

The reputed powers of the old charters, as interpreted by the Lords, were still being exercised well into the first quarter of the fourteenth century. On many manors the serfs found themselves liable to seizure and punishment under such quasi-legal rights. An example of such malpractice is hanging for theft.

Some Lords had, or assumed that they had, rights of 'infangenethef' or 'outfagenethef' as defined above. But there was a legal proviso to such rights that the thief had to be taken 'hand-having' or 'back-bearing;' he must be prosecuted by the loser of the goods, and further that the Coroner must be present during the proceedings.

Many Lords did not bother overmuch about such details. As far as they were concerned the man was a thief and had been captured, where and how was of little consequence so they hung him! The court rolls were brief and to the point in recording such matters and the details of such trials usually end with the words '... let him have a priest.' But the power to erect a gallows and to hang criminals was essentially a Royal prerogative and the Crown gradually sought to take back into its own hands all such privileges which the Lord had usurped by ambitious interpretation of their charter rights.

The Coroners

It was the business of the Coroners to see that the Royal rights were not infringed and that the property of condemned felons was not appropriated by the manorial Lords but duly paid over to the Crown. Several such officers were appointed in each Shire and they were required to attend all sessions of the itinerant justices and bring their records with them for inspection. The Coroner's Courts were 'courts of record,' i.e. the written accounts of their proceedings were held to be authoritative and acceptable in evidence, hence their great importance.

In all cases where a Manorial Court applied the death sentence the presence of the King's Coroner was essential. Thus, to some extent, the manorial jurisdiction was kept in some check by this official. Even if a thief was taken in the act he could not, without considerable risk to the Lord concerned, be hanged in the absence of the coroner.

The Court Baron

By the late thirteenth century there were two main types of manorial jurisdiction in existence. The first of these arose directly out of the Lords' seigniorial rights as feudal Barons and gave them powers to administer their estates and control their tenants. During the sixteenth century, lawyers made a distinction between the Court Baron, held for the manorial freemen, and the Court Customary, which controlled the serfs. In practice no such separation ever existed and the Manor Courts performed both functions at the same time and place.

Courts Leet and View of Frankpledge

The second type of jurisdiction which was conferred on selected Lords of the manor, was the right to hold Courts Leet and 'View of Frankpledge.' These rights gave jurisdiction over petty criminal offences committed by the manorial tenants, and others, within the manorial boundaries. Such rights were held to be 'regalities' - i.e. they could only properly be exercised by those Lords who had been granted a specific franchise by the King. Without such franchises these matters were only within the competence of the Royal jurisdiction - e.g. the Hundred Courts.

Originally 'Leet' and 'View of Frankpledge' were quite separate functions. The former dealt with petty criminal and civil matters, while the latter was a court held periodically to examine the effective working of the system of 'Frankpledge.' This dated back to Saxon times when each area was divided into groups of ten or twelve households, known as tithings, in which members were held corporately responsible for the behaviour of each other, with matters being regulated at the View of Frankpledge. Over many years these two functions became so associated with each other that the Court Leet performed both functions at one and the same time and place.

In practice the Leet and Manor Courts were usually held together and although separate records were sometimes kept this was not universally the case. Thus much confusion arose because one and the same court often seemed to be dealing with matters arising out of both seigniorial rights and Royal franchises.

The system of 'Frankpledge' dated back to Saxon times when each area was divided into groups of ten or twelve households, known as tithings, in which members were held corporately responsible for the behaviour of each other,

It was the business of the thirteenth century lawyers to explain this confusion and the courts increasingly differentiated between the Lords' feudal rights and Royal franchises. Very gradually, out of a confused and contentious past, the law became clearer and more certain.

The peasant then, rich or poor, the serfs, and to a limited extent the freemen, were bound to attend the Manor Courts. However, it was entirely a matter of chance with what powers they found them endowed or whether their Lords were mild, grasping, weak or strong! Conditions varied greatly, even between adjoining manors, and uniformity of administration was a rarity.

Frequency of Manor Courts Sittings

The peasant suitors of the Manor Courts were bound by ancient custom to attend 'from three weeks to three weeks.' The records show a bewildering variety of practice in this respect. The actual frequency of the manorial court sessions could be anything from twice a year to once every two weeks! As with most manorial affairs local needs and custom were the determining factors.

Prior to the year 1234 the Manor Courts were mostly held every two weeks. However, an ordinance of that year said they should not be held more frequently than every three weeks, but this decree was never strictly enforced. On some manors, following the combination of the seigniorial courts with Courts Leet and View of Frankpledge, it became convenient to hold just two courts a year thus conforming with the second reissue of Magna Carter in 1217 which decreed that, among other things, the Leet and View of Frankpledge were to be held twice yearly.

No doubt the reason why the Lords made use of the term 'three weeks to three weeks' was that once this was on the record they could interpret it as strictly or leniently as they wished and they knew that the lawyers would always uphold them. But whether the courts sat frequently or seldom, it was essential that the suitors should know exactly when they had to attend and various methods were devised to ensure this. On some manors the date of the next court was announced at the end of each session, on others it was always held on a prearranged day each month.

The latter type of arrangements mostly prevailed on the smaller estates where the Lords ran their own courts. Those Lords with the largest estates, often consisting of many manors, usually found it necessary to employ stewards. In these circumstances the Lords had to consider the most economical way of proceeding. hence the courts were not held with the same regularity, or frequency, as those on the smaller manors.

In the latter circumstances the best they could do was to give 'reasonable summons.' Sometimes this amounted to as much as three days notice, at others only one day was given, and sometimes the long-suffering serf was warned in the middle of the night of a court to be held the next morning!

However, the serfs and the freemen were not treated the same in this respect and the freeman was much more difficult to control. During the thirteenth century, if a Lord wanted 'suit of court' from a free tenant he had to make this absolutely clear when he granted the land. otherwise the accepted doctrine seems to have been that a free tenant was only bound to attend his Lord's court for matters of Royal concern - i.e. when police or criminal matters were involved. The Statute of Marlborough 1267 clarified the matter thus: "No freeholder is bound to suit his Lord's court unless this was imposed on him by the terms of his charter, or was done (i.e. was customary) before King Henry III went to Brittany in the year 1230." If a Lord required more suit of court than this from a freeman he had to bargain for it when he granted the land.

The court of the Abbot of St. Albans was held '... under the ash-tree in the middle courtyard of the Abbey.'

In those cases where actual notice of the court sessions were necessary, it was given in a variety of ways. Sometimes an announcement was made in the church, and on some manors notice was given at the tenant's houses by the beadles. Sometimes it was the duty of one of the serfs to give such notice to the rest of the peasantry. In cases of uncertainty the ultimate responsibility rested with the bailiff or reeves to see that all the peasants received proper notice of imminent court sessions.

Location of the Manor Courts

By law the Manor Court had to be held within the boundaries of the manor and its location was usually fixed by custom. Some courts were held in the open air as in Knyttington Manor in Berkshire, where it was held '... in a certain green place over against the house of Hugh de Gardin when it was fine, and in wet weather, by leave of the bailiff in the manor house or in that on one of the tenants.' In Moulsham Hall in Essex it was also held in the open, outside the manor house under the 'Court Oak,' and at Little Leigh in Essex, the court was held on 'Court Hill.' The court of the Abbot of St. Albans was held '... under the ash-tree in the middle courtyard of the Abbey.'

Another common location for the courts was in the hall of the manor house. This was probably the origin of 'Hallmote' - i.e. 'hall-meeting' - as an alternative name for the Manor Courts.

It would therefore appear that the assertion that the manorial hall was the only right place to hold the Manor Court seems much too rigid. In fact the only 'right place' was where-ever ancient custom decreed, and any variation of custom was an assertion of the Lord's will.

The Manor Court in Session

The Manor Courts were sometimes presided over by the Lords themselves, although more often this function was performed on the Lord's behalf by their stewards. When the court was in session the president sat at the desk on a raised dais overlooking the court, and their clerks sat beside them. As the president took his place on the dais the beadle called for silence and then, with a single cry of "Oyez" if it was a Manorial Court, or a triple "Oyez" if it was a Leet Court, he called on all who owed suit of court to "draw nigh and be heard." The proceedings then began and were recorded, item by item, in the Court Roll by the clerk.

The first items to be dealt with were the excuses for absences - known as the 'essoins.' The absentee had to arrange for his excuse, whether verbal or written, to be presented to the court on his behalf and this was recorded and numbered against his name on the court roll. This entry protected him from a fine. The 'essoin' had to be made for some good reason, not given out of mere caprice. Once any suitor had three 'essoins' enrolled against him he was brought before the court and had to justify each absence. If he succeeded all was well and he could start again, otherwise he was fined.

The Juries and the Dooms

Early in the proceedings the jury, or juries, were sworn in. However, these were juries of accusation not judgement, and they reported to the whole body of the court. It was this latter body, which was composed of all those owing 'suit of court' and known as the 'tota curia,' who gave the final 'dooms' or verdicts. In effect it could be said that these juries performed most of the functions of the modern-day prosecutors and witnesses; while the 'tota curia,' rather like the modern jury, gave its judgements based on matters of fact; and the Lords or their stewards were the judges.

Where it was appropriate a president of a court could accept a 'doom' given exclusively by the freemen, if it only affected the freeholders. On the other hand, a 'doom' given by the villeins alone was equally acceptable in those cases where only the 'custom of the manor' was involved. To distinguish the latter restricted 'doom' from those given by the 'tota curia,' they were enrolled on the Court Rolls as being given by 'omnes libre tenentes,' or by 'omnes nativi,' respectively. Thus it can be said, in theory at least, that the manorial tenants, both bond and free, were entitled to the judgement of their neighbours as well as that of the Lord's stewards.

This ancient custom of the manorial villeins being the makers of 'dooms' in the Manor Court lasted throughout the Middle Ages. However, during the thirteenth century the manorial courts gradually made more use of the jury system. Of course this was an imitation of the Royal Courts into which the jury of presentment had been introduce by King Henry II in 1166.

This copying of the King's Courts arose largely because so many Lords had been granted Royal franchises to hold Courts Leet and 'View of Frankpledge.' These latter courts were held to be, in the strict legal sense, King's court's and therefore they were required, by the law of 1166, to empanel twelve men juries of presentment to enquire into offences against the King's peace.

Naturally these juries did not confine themselves strictly to matters affecting the Kings peace and franchises and soon they were making further enquiries on the Lord's behalf. Thus, although the juries of presentment were supposed to be concerned only with offences against the franchises, in practice many matters of seigniorial concern came to be listed as capable of being properly dealt with in the Courts Leet.

Examples of such matters are abuses by manorial officials; usurping of hunting and fishing rights; encroachment on the Lords' lands; marriage of the villeins' daughters or education of their sons without proper licence, etc.

Juries of Inquisition

As well as the above accusatory juries there also developed the juries of inquisition whose business was to enquire into manorial offences and matters concerning the working of the manor. These juries were of variable size and composition and were usually chosen so as to represent all sections of the manor.

The juries of inquisition were very often ad hoc bodies and came to be used more and more to make sworn inquisitions as to verifiable matters of fact. Their size could vary from five to twelve members and, where very important matters were involved, could be composed of up to as many as twenty-four persons.

During the thirteenth century the manorial courts gradually made more use of the jury system.

The duties of the juries of inquisition were many and varied. They had to enquire into matters of fact and declare what was the 'custom of the manor;' they deliberated in disputes between tenants and returned the verdicts upon which the court acted; they made surveys and reported on ancient rights; they were empowered to draw up by-laws for the regulation of the common fields and meadows; and to make inquisitions in to the state of various buildings and the condition of manorial buildings.

The juries of inquisition, were a very practical and direct means of enquiry into any matters of fact that were in dispute and were widely used by both the Lords of the Manor and their tenants. However, when the tenant made use of the jury they were charged for the privilege. The sums involved could vary from 6d. (2.5p) to 6s. 8d. (33p), considerable sums in those times, but it was considered to be money well spent because not only did the successful litigant get a clear, enforceable decision but the verdict was enrolled in the court records and henceforth became 'custom of the manor.'

The Jurors

There is no way of discovering exactly how the juries were chosen. They are generally written of as being 'elected' but nothing is known of how this was done. It seems much more probable that those who were liable for such service were somehow pre-selected because most court rolls contain long lists of names headed 'Nomina Juratorum.' Thus ad hoc juries were probably selected, and sworn in, from these lists early in the proceedings of each court session.

The personal status of the jurors and what qualified them to serve are equally obscure. In the early days the juries were composed of both freemen and serfs. However, the freemen soon challenged the rights of the Lords to compel them to serve on the same juries as the serfs. In the Courts Leet, which were in effect Royal Courts, the Lords as the King's agents could compel the freemen to serve on the juries of presentation, as could the King's Justices in the Shire and Hundred Courts.

In those courts which were confined to dealing with manorial business it is doubtful whether a Lord could legally compel a freeholder tenant to take an oath as a juryman - although many freemen, no doubt, took such oaths sooner than be in conflict with their Lords! Of course an exception to the latter rule was where a freeman owed 'suit of court,' either by agreement with his Lord or because his land had its origin in villeinage. Such free tenants as these could be compelled to serve as jurymen in the Manorial Courts.

Throughout the thirteenth and fourteenth centuries, there was a growing reluctance by the freemen to serve on mixed juries with the serfs. In course of time manors used two systems of juries, one composed of freemen, the other of serfs.

On some manors it was the tithing-men who acted as a jury of presentment at the 'View of Frankpledge' and, after they had presented their charges, a jury of twelve freemen were sworn in to declare that the tithing-men had done everything in order and had omitted nothing. By the year 1390 most Manor courts were using juries composed entirely of freemen to present offences against the franchises, while separate juries, composed of bondsmen, presented other offences and elected the manorial officers. By 1410 the juries both of presentment and inquisition, were dealing only with their peers.

The jury system was far from perfect and many complaints of incompetence were made. Some litigants went so far as to declare that justice was impossible because the Lord's men packed the juries! However, more often it was tardy verdicts of neglect of duty that was complained of. Very often later events brought new facts to light and the wretched jurymen were fined, either for failing to investigate hard enough or for concealing the truth. Thus, taken by and large, a juryman's lot was not a happy one!

The Lords were accustomed to using their courts as a source of income, and fining jurors was one of the ways they used to increase their funds.

Jury Fines

The Lords were accustomed to using their courts as a source of income, and fining jurors was one of the ways they used to increase their funds. The juries were fined for concealment of marriages, sales of land, encroachments on the Lord's land, etc.; even although their offences were probably only carelessness. Uniformity and consistency were strictly enforced and the coercion and punishment of dissenting jurors seems to have been frequent. Fines for contradicting fellow jurors were also common, and offenders were not only fined by the Lords but could also be acted against by those litigants who lost prestige because of their lack of unanimity.

The deliberations of the juries were of great interest to the manorial tenants and great care had to be taken to keep them secret so as to avoid further litigation. It was commonplace for such secrecy to be broken which resulted, as always, in fines being imposed on the long-suffering jury! On the other hand their verdicts often gave rise to violent expressions of opinion with men standing up in court and upbraiding the jury. Such conduct inevitably resulted in yet more fines!

The Jurisdiction of the Manor Courts

The matters which a Manor Court, possessed of the fullest franchises and charters, was legally competent to deal with can be classified under three headings: manorial administration; minor offences against law and order; and breach of the King's peace. This includes all those matters which were under the undisputed jurisdiction of the Lords of the Manor, e.g. - the regulation and enforcement of labour services; the punishment of all kinds of trespass; the overcrowding of commons; the too frequent taking of wood or turfs; trespass by animals on the Lord's waste etc. Also included under this heading was the transfer of all land tenures that were held in villeinage, and also the sale of freehold land if the Lord's interests were impaired thereby.

Regulations for the control of the open fields and commons came under the court's economic jurisdiction. Control of the serf's freedom to marry, take holy orders, or leave the manor, being matters vitally concerning the working of the Lord's demesne, also concerned the court, as did offences against morality by the peasants. For example, if a serf was successfully prosecuted by an ecclesiastical court for adultery and was fined by it, in theory he had lost something which belonged to his Lord. In the same way a woman serf who lost her virginity was of less value, and was therefore fined for depreciating her Lord's property!

Manorial Offences Against the Law

For practical purposes the Lords had to be allowed to deal with minor offences against the law because they effected the smooth working of manorial life. Violence, as long as it was not too extreme, was punishable by the court, e.g. attacks on manorial officers, threats and mild assaults on neighbours, etc. More serious offences, such as driving off a neighbour's cattle, or stealing another's crops, were also dealt with. Civil disputes between tenants were also decided by the court with both sides stating their case and then a verdict given, either by jury or the whole court.

Breach of contract and failure to fulfil obligations were also considered and damages assessed. Slander also came before the Manor Court and wounded pride claimed, and sometimes received, monetary compensation. Not only could a tenant be cheapened by unfair criticism, but even his beasts or crops could be and men were fined for vilifying another man's pig, or for defaming his crop so that he lost the sale of it!

Breaches of the King's Peace

At manorial level, only those Lords who had been granted Royal Charters to hold Leet Courts and View of Frankpledge were competent to deal with offences against the King's peace. In the absence of such charters these offences came under the sole jurisdiction of the King's Justices in the Shire and Hundred Courts.

The scope of the manorial Courts Leet was defined in the 'Articles of the View of Frankpledge' which were contained in their Charters of grant.

In the Courts Leet the sworn juries, or the 'tithing men,' were required to make their presentments concerning all kinds of crimes from brewing without a licence to open murder! Personal injuries; infringements of the highway; harbouring strangers; using false weights and measures; frequenting taverns at night; poaching; clipping coins; and many similar petty offences; were considered by the juries, and the offenders presented for justice to be done.

Manor Court Fines

As well as providing great prestige and the means to punish transgressors, the Manor Courts also provided an important part of the Lords' incomes, especially those Lords who had franchises to hold Leet Courts. In general the fines were imposed at the discretion of the Lords or their officials. However, it was accepted that they should be assessed mercifully and 'affeered,' i.e. agreed, by the peers of the victim. Thus the culprits had both the custom of the manor and the clemency of his fellows to rely on.

There is no way of assessing the values of the Lords' incomes from the Manor Courts. Sometimes they were trivial, at others substantial, and the size of the manor had little to do with the amount of the income obtained from its court. However, the incomes obtained from such sources were usually sufficiently valuable to warrant a separate paragraph in the annual accounts submitted by the bailiffs.

Powers of the Manor Courts

During the thirteenth and fourteenth centuries the courts rapidly developed in technical complexity. Men found that they could avoid charges by means of some technical point of pleading. For example, a plaintiff who failed to name the day or hour in which certain goods were stolen from him had his plea rejected.

A plaintiff charged a defendant with assault and stealing his bow and arrows and the defendant pleaded that he was not bound to answer because he was charged with two offences, one of which may have been true and the other false! Many examples of such pleadings are to be found in contemporary law books which illustrate the complexity of the law even as early as in the fourteenth century.

The medieval Manor Courts were often comparatively powerless to enforce their own orders. Many court rolls record that such and such a thing was ordered to be done 'as hath oftimes been commanded,' and often the very same entry appears in the records of the next session. Men who had fled the manor could not be found and brought back and the power of the Courts often seems curiously feeble, even when dealing with serfs.

For example, men 'forgot' court orders to clear away nuisances, replace boundary stones, or repair their dilapidated houses. The bailiffs reported such omissions at subsequent sessions and the orders were repeated. This process continued until either the serfs acted or the bailiffs grew tired and gave up! Clever men could avoid making any answer to the Courts for considerable periods of time by means of 'essoins.'

Whatever their weakness, the Manor Courts were useful and worthwhile institutions, and not merely a means whereby the Lords could control and punish their tenants! They were also great barriers against violent changes of manorial policy. In the court rolls were recorded new interpretations or newly created precedents concerning the 'custom of the manor.' As were the findings of the juries regarding such things as the liability of the 'suitors of the Court' to render work services and their determinations as to the boundaries of the Lords' demesne lands and their own fields, etc.

It is true that the Manor Courts, except when they functioned under Royal Franchises as Leet Courts, were not Courts of Record as recognised by the King's Justices. However, they were true courts of record so far as the serfs were concerned, and they were constantly ready to pay for searches of the rolls so that the truth of falsity of their claims could be established. When serfs came into court to take over or surrender land the scribes entered the details on the rolls and they were often asked for copies of these entries so all doubts regarding the tenancies might be avoided.

The Manor Courts provided the peasants with a speedy and comparatively inexpensive way of obtaining redress for all kinds of wrongs. The activities of lawyers were largely, but not totally, excluded from these courts and, in general, their procedures were simple enough to be understood by most of the peasants. This patriarchal system prevailed throughout most of the middle ages and men resorted to these courts with at least a reasonable chance of receiving the protection of their Lords where appropriate.

The King's Courts were remote, difficult to access, costly and daunting to the simple peasants. Manor Courts on the other hand were readily available. In them the peasants could plead redress for almost every kind of wrong and could claim the 'doom' of the court, that is to say the verdict of his fellow peasants, before the judgement of their Lords was pronounced. A great disadvantage of the King's Courts, so far as the serfs were concerned, was that whereas they had the protection of common law in them, they were barred from acting against their Lords.

The Manor Courts survived until the first quarter of the twentieth century. They usually operated in close co-operation with the parochial authorities and their function was to preserve manorial custom and to regulate matters between the Lords of the Manor and their freeholders, copyholders and other tenants. After the reforms of the Law of Property Act of 1925, which converted all copyholds into freeholds, the Courts fell into decline.

The Serf's Long Road to Freedom

From 1066 until the Peasants Revolt in 1381 the majority of the people in England were not free. However, throughout this period constant efforts were being made by the serfs to obtain their freedom. Everywhere men were at work seeking to break the bonds which bound them to the land they were born on. Although, evidence of their efforts is scarce: what is certain is that in 1350 half the population of England were serfs and in 1600 there were none! There are several major factors which caused the final demise of serfdom - the scarcity of labour after the Black Death in 1349; new methods of land leasing; the attractions of life in towns; and the growing belief among the Lords of the Manor that money rents were more advantageous to them than the ancient feudal service dues.

Ways Serfs Could Gain Their Freedom

There were a number of different ways serfs could lessen their servile conditions. For example, they could commute their week-works, boon-works, tallages and other servile burdens for additional rents, known as 'quit-rents.' However, complete freedom was more difficult to attain, and the most straightforward way of achieving this was to obtain from their Lords, by purchase or agreement, release from their bondage - i.e. freedom by grant of manumission.

Another widely used route to freedom was to run away to the nearest town and seek protection within its walls. If such runaway serfs could avoid recapture for one year and a day they could thereafter legally claim complete freedom. Lastly there was flight without definite objective, other than the vague hope of better things to sustain them. By all these various ways the serfs gradually became free.

The 'extents' contain evidence of the various efforts of the unfree to shake off their servile chains. Naturally the earliest way of escaping serfdom was by flight. To a large number of serfs it must have seemed that any kind of change in their lives could have been for the better! However, to leave the manor without the Lords' permission was too drastic for the majority as it meant leaving behind everything they had ever known. Yet, in spite of the risks, practically every manor in England knew of someone who had absconded and was living as a free man in a nearby town, or was farming his own acres as a free man on some distant manor.

Many could recall how a serf had run away and had refused every order of the Manor Court to return. Every Lord of the Manor knew how hard it was to find a runaway serf once he had got a few miles away and mindful of these facts the majority of Lords, slowly and reluctantly, came to terms with the aspirations of their serfs.

The serfs' great desire for freedom was motivated by two main factors. The first was their dislike of the fixed works and services they owed their Lords, which were often demanded most heavily at times when their own crops needed attention. The other factor was their deep hatred of the tallages and similar charges and burdens that bore all the most obvious stigma of serfdom.

Quit Rents

The serfs dislike of fixed works and services is very easy to understand. However, views on this subject were often mutual and the Lords on many manors actively encouraged their serfs to commute such services for quit-rents. The medieval handbook of estate husbandry, 'Walter of Henley,' tells the Lords - 'customary servants neglect their work, and it is necessary always to guard against their fraud!' Thus many Lords concluded that they would get better value from hired labourers than from unwilling serfs and used the money received from quit-rents to pay for such hired hands.

In general it was the 'week-works' that were the most easily commuted because they went on throughout the whole year and the Lords could plan to hire labour to cover any shortfall. However, the 'boon-works' at harvest times were not so easily commutable because it was too great an advantage to the Lords to have their labour both on the spot and available immediately the time was right to begin to gather in their crops.

The method and pace of progress from serfdom to freedom varied greatly from manor to manor. In general the commutation of the serfs' service burdens was probably due more to the local, personal, and monetary needs of the Lords than it was to any far-reaching national causes - especially prior to 1350 and the effects of the Black Death on the national economy. The fact remains that once the serfs had persuaded their Lords to accept quit-rents in lieu of services, their road to freedom was at least in sight although complete emancipation was still to be achieved.

Manumission

From time to time the Lords found that it was in their own best interests to free some of their serfs. The charters by which such freedoms were granted were often masterpieces of hypocrisy containing long recitals of meaningless phrases such as - 'it is pious and meritorious to restore men to that state of natural freedom ... which belonged to all human beings.' However, these time worn phrases were often copied by the scribes from earlier charters and were rendered meaningless by constant repetition and habitual usage over the years. In most of the charters of emancipation that have survived, the Lords' self interests is apparent and they very often exacted handsome payments for the enfranchisements they agreed to confer on their serfs.

When dealing with manumission the Lords tried to get the best of both worlds. Their charters were embellished with words of God, but their account rolls meticulously recorded the monetary gain obtained by them! The serfs soon found that freedom was not to be had for the mere asking! Indeed, if it had not been for the Lords' constant shortage of money the serfs might well have longed for freedom for a much longer time without more than a few of them ever achieving it. However, the growing love of luxury by the aristocracy, Royal taxes imposed for various purposes, wars at home and overseas, and the medieval Lords' money problems, all helped the serfs towards their eventual freedom.

There are many cases whereby the Lords entered into agreements with their serfs to release them from their servile duties in return for annual quit-rents. By these means whole villages won for themselves conditions that almost amounted to emancipation for, although the Lords often retained certain services, such as ploughing and harvesting, once the serfs had paid their yearly rents and quit-rents they were their own masters. No doubt such agreements were to the mutual advantage of both parties, and there can be little doubt that these changes encouraged the serfs on neighbouring manors to strive for like privileges when they observed what freedoms others had won.

Real unimpeachable freedom by charter, however, was usually gained by direct action on the part of the serfs themselves. We can imagine them saving, bit by bit, enough to offer their Lord a fair sum for their charters of manumission, The medieval records are full of entries showing the moneys received from such grants, and the sums involved are sometimes quite large. However, these receipts are usually all that is recorded and the willingness or otherwise of the Lords to manumit and their reasons for doing so are seldom stated.

Conditional Manumission

Even when the Lords did consent to grant freedom they were not always willing to forego all of their seigniorial rights over the serfs concerned. For example, the Prior of Bath manumitted a serf on condition that he served the priory for the rest of his life in his craft of plumber and glazier; the Chapter of Canterbury confirmed a manumission, by the Archbishop, of a bondman and his sons, with the proviso that the youngest son should remain on the manor as a serf with the family fixtures and livestock; and the Bishop of Winchester granted a charter to one John de Wambleworth and his heirs, but it did not excuse them from 'suit of court,' or payment of 'pannage' and 'heriots.'

There are many other examples similar to these and everywhere the Lords were only willing to allow just so much freedom as suited their purposes; and by only partially yielding to the serfs' aspirations, they contrived to 'have their cake and eat it!'

Constructibe Manumission

Throughout the twelfth and thirteenth centuries the lawyers were far from certain of exactly how the law stood regarding manumission, One contemporary lawyer, Glanvill (c1187), considered that all serfs were incapable of buying their own freedom because legally they owned nothing - everything they possessed belonged ultimately to their Lords. This technicality could be readily overcome by the use a third party to act as the purchaser of the serf's freedom; the money used in such transactions appeared to belong to the third party, whereas, of course, it was provided by the freed serf! By the mid thirteenth century things had changed and there were many cases of serfs successfully purchasing their freedom with their own money.

The law on manumission was complicated and remained in a state of continual flux throughout the 13th century. As well as the difficulties arising out of manumission by charter, the lawyers argued about certain acts by the Lords in their dealings with their serfs, which some lawyers held to imply a recognition of free status; this was termed 'constructive manumission.' Of these arguments the most important was whether or not by entering into an agreement with a mere serf a Lord conferred freedom on him - by treating a serf as a free man did the Lord make him free?

By the end of the thirteenth century a great many things were taken by the lawyers in the King's Courts to imply constructive manumission which were best summed up by the lawyer Bracton (c1250) whose advice on this matter was as follows :

'A villein will become free if his Lord grants land to him and his heirs, whether or not he pays homage to the Lord. A bondman becomes free if he marries his Lady, or a bondwoman if she marries her Lord, and their descendants shall for ever be free. A bondman will be free if his Lord has acknowledged him so to be in any Court of Record (i.e. a Leet Court or any other King's Court). Likewise, a serf shall be made free by any writing of his Lord (e.g. in a deed) which implies that the Lord has, for himself and his heirs, quit-claimed to the serf, and his heirs, all his seigniorial rights held by reason of the serf's bondage. So shall a serf be free where he can prove by the record of a King's Court that his Lord has knowingly suffered him to serve on juries or inquisitions on that court as a freeman.'

This is a comprehensive statement of the medieval law concerning constructive manumission and no doubt it assisted a number of men to win their freedom.

The Attraction of the Towns

The majority of men, once they had won their freedom, had no great desire to leave their villages. Once free of the yoke of servitude most men were content to live as peasants and cultivate their fields and closes. For many years they had longed to call their cottages and chattels their own and work their fields in their own way.

However, there were some important exceptions to this 'stay put' tendency and outside influences induced some men to seek their freedom in the towns.

Without doubt, the serf's long struggle towards freedom was much encouraged and sustained by the freedoms that had been gained by the burgesses who dwelt in the Boroughs. From the earliest times these townsmen had set an example to their unfree brothers on the manors, and the towns played an inestimable part in the eventual emancipation of the manorial serfs.

The burgesses often lived in houses clustered round some Bishop's palace, or lying in the shadow of some feudal Baron's castle. Originally they had been subject to services, tallages and heriots, just like the serfs on the manors. However, unlike their manorial cousins the burgesses had realised at an early stage that their servile status was not inevitable and that means could be found of overcoming seigniorial exploitation.

As towns became increasingly attractive, by reason of their more civilised lifestyle and security, they attracted some of the richest, intelligent, and most enterprising men in the Kingdom. These people came into contact with traders and others from foreign parts, and from them learned new and disturbing ideas. These included the steps which had been taken by the men of Rouen, and other towns, to gain freedom from the control of feudal Lords. Gradually there arose among the burgesses an imperious need to be the masters of their own towns and they agitated for their freedom.

The Free Boroughs

They soon found that freedom was not to be had merely for the asking. Charters were granted to the boroughs as a result of a multitude of reasons, but in general the towns only won their freedom at the expense of much gold! Of course, many Lords realised that it was very much to their own advantage to establish free boroughs. They knew that such freed franchises bought them considerable profit from fairs, markets, tolls etc., and more than compensated them for the loss of the services of their serfs.

Without doubt, the serf's long struggle towards freedom was much encouraged and sustained by the freedoms that had been gained by the burgesses who dwelt in the Boroughs.

However, in the overwhelming majority of cases it was the need for money that prompted the Lords to agree to the establishment of the free boroughs. Nevertheless, they were usually reluctant to abdicate their powers and seldom gave up all their rights at one strike! Thus, in the earlier charters, the Lords usually reserved to themselves some of their old feudal rights. But, over the years, the burgesses took advantage of every opportunity to bargain for further privileges in order to enlarge the scope of their Charters, and eventually the boroughs acquired virtual self-government. This was a slow process, however, and the actual rate of progress varied as local circumstances dictated. In 1086 there had been 96 charter boroughs in existence, by the year 1100 this number had increased to 166.

The monetary needs of the nobles, when setting out on the crusades, often provided the burgesses with good opportunities to bargain for improvements to their charters! Also, in those many boroughs where the King was the overlord, greater freedom from Royal interference in local affairs was often obtained for similar reasons. This is especially true of King Richard I (1189-99) and John (1199-1216), who were both in constant need of money for crusades, foreign wars, or ransom! Thus, by these and various other means, the charter boroughs gradually became more powerful and much richer.

The Burgesses

Regardless of the seigniorial rights that were often reserved to the Lords in the early charters, the status of the burgesses was, from the outset, superior to the servile position of the manorial villeins. The advantages of the burgesses over the unfree villeins was firstly, their tenures were not at the 'will of the lord,' as were the villein's cottages and closes. They could dispose of their town houses as they wished and almost as easily as they could their chattels.

Next, they were free from such death duties as 'heriot' and 'mortuary' and by-laws fixed and regulated their services, if any. They had their own Borough Courts and their disputes were tried and decided by their fellow townsmen - with no Lord to have the last word! Also there were usually by-laws whereas there was no such legal limits to the fines that could be imposed by the Manor Courts.

Lastly, in most cases, the burgesses were free from paying tolls in the borough market place and very often on all such other estates as were possessed by the Lords.

In fact, the privileges enjoyed by the burgesses were one of the major determinates that resulted in the eventual emancipation of the English countryside. The boroughs, with their charters and freedoms, were a constant challenge. To the villeins they were a perpetual reminder of their servile status as compared to their more fortunate brothers in the charter towns, and to the Lords of the Manor they presented an ever-present threat to the seigniorial autocracy.

Consequently, in order to retain their serfs on the manors, many Lords were obliged to grant conditions approximating those enjoyed by the burgesses in the nearby boroughs.

Borough Charters

Local self-government by the boroughs was rarely fully achieved by the first charter, such status usually evolved as the result of a long struggle. Of course the process usually had the effect of increasing the personal freedom of the burgesses be releasing them from such servile obligations that had been reserved by the Lords in the original charters. In most cases, therefore, it can be said that the free burgesses of the thirteenth century were descended from villeins of the eleventh and twelfth. In most boroughs it took several charters, and much money, to finally eliminate all the old feudal servitudes.

In some places, however, the serfs were transformed into freeholding burgesses at the stroke of a pen! For example, the Earl of Derby founded his borough of Higham Ferrers on St. Gregory's Day 1251. Ninety-two men, whose names are recorded in the charter, therefore awoke that morning as serfs and by evening were all free men, '... so that from them and their families, with all their lands, tenements and chattels, the Earl and his heirs could not from henceforth have or exact any servitude from them or their issue.' A number of such boroughs founded in the twelfth and thirteenth centuries had similar histories. In general however, progress towards borough status was more gradual and in most cases full freedom took the burgesses many years to obtain.

The serfs always had a remote chance that their Lords, for one reason or another, might enfranchise their village and convert them into charter boroughs. However, such events were rare and many of these hastily created charter towns later relapsed into serfdom again.

Nevertheless, the freedom that existed in the towns provided a constant incentive to the more adventurous manorial serfs to seek their fortunes therein. They were also, by their example, a spur to the unfree tenants on the manors to seek similar privileges and improved status.

The serfs always had a remote chance that their Lords might enfranchise their village. However, such events were rare and many of these hastily created charter towns later relapsed into serfdom again.

The Flight to the Boroughs

The contrast between the status of the serfs and the burgesses was at its most conspicuous where manors and the boroughs had adjoining boundaries. Naturally such serfs, burdened with innumerable obligations to their Lords, looked with envy on their neighbours in the adjoining fields who were free of such servitude. Small wonder then that many of them yielded to temptation and crossed the boundary to seek the freedom, safe shelter, and often the welcome of the nearby town.

The above trend is reflected in the medieval records of most of the charter boroughs, which show that a constant influx of outsiders was being received. The other side of the picture is revealed in the court rolls of the nearby manors. Again and again men are reported as being fugitives dwelling in nearby towns, and although repeated orders are given that they be brought back the towns continued to protect them. After a year or so these ineffective demands cease to be made and the names of the fugitives drop out of the rolls.

The Extension of the Boroughs

The ambitions of the burgesses often had the side effect of helping to free some of their manorial neighbours. This came about because once they were secure themselves they soon found their boroughs were too small and cast envious eyes on some manor whose fields adjoined their town.

For example, in 1256 the burgesses of Scarborough found themselves cramped and obtained a charter from King Henry III for the increase of their borough to absorb the King's own manor of Wallesgrave (Palsgrave) '... with all its appurtenances and 60 acres in the fields of Scarborough'.

Thus, although the motives of the burgesses of Scarborough had been entirely self-seeking, they had effectively transformed the serfs of Palsgrave into burgesses of Scarborough entitled to all the freedoms and privileges of its charter. Similar developments occurred throughout England and the burgesses, for security, extended their defensive walls so as to enclose the newly added lands. Thus protected the new burgesses were secure from any danger of reversion to their original servile status.

The Creation of New Towns

The enfranchisement of their villages, desertion to the towns, and the absorption of their manors into boroughs, were not the only means by which serfs obtained burgess rights. There was another important way in which this desirable status could be achieved. For some time, especially during the reign of Edward I, constantly recurring opportunities to become burgesses were provided by the creation of new towns.

In those charters where Lords of the Manor granted borough status to whole villages, it was only the lucky few who lived in the village at the time of its emancipation who benefited. However, the new boroughs were deliberately created in places where previously nothing had existed, and thus greater numbers reaped the benefit.

As it was necessary to attract settlers to such places from far and wide, all men, including serfs, were welcome. The King (for they were mostly Royal creations) offered land and burgess rights to everyone who was willing to take up residence in the new boroughs.

As a first step in their creation, the King appointed officials to lay out the new boroughs with sufficient streets; adequate sites for a market place and a church; and plots for the use of merchants and others. The King then granted a charter to the new town and declared himself willing to grant merchants, and others willing to take them, possession of the town lands for building and dwelling purposes. An example of such a creation is Rhuddlan in Clwyd. This town was situated in the Welsh borderlands which were in need of repopulation after King Edward I's conquest of Wales c1284.

To achieve this restoration, the King decreed that all men wishing to become farmers or grantees of lands in those devastated districts should apply to the King's officers at Shrewsbury or Hereford, while those desiring the security of living in a town should apply to the Justices in Chester who had the power to 'assign places in Rhuddlan to all who desire to receive and hold the same from the King'. Other examples of new boroughs are Chard in Somerset and Hull in Yorkshire. There is nothing in the charters to suggest that the serfs were in any way barred from making application.

A Year and a Day

All chartered towns therefore offered great opportunity and advantages. However, so far as the runaway serfs were concerned the mere passing through the town gate was not, in itself, sufficient to gain them their freedom. For instance, during the first four days of their absence, their Lords could pursue them and forceable return them to the manors from where-ever they found them.

As the runaway serfs were concerned the mere passing through the town gate was not, in itself, sufficient to gain them their freedom.

However, after that period had lapsed it was another matter because by then the serfs were considered to be free by 'possession of liberty' and the Lords could not repossess them without a court order. Therefore, serfs were not really free at this stage, and their mere assumption of liberty, which could be revoked by the justices, did not bring them the complete freedom they desired.

Without doubt, the towns were a considerable help to the runaway serfs in their quest for personal liberty, for by living within the walls of a chartered borough for a year and a day, they acquired a certain degree of freedom. Simple residence in a town, however, rarely gave the serfs all the burgess privileges that were granted by the charters.

The notion of freedom by residence had its origins in the ancient Anglo-Saxon laws, which had been continued after the Norman Conquest, known as the 'Willelmi Articuli Retracti.' The appropriate section of these laws, as written down c1200, reads - "If serfs have remained a year and a day without being claimed in our (i.e. the King's) cities or our walled boroughs or in our castles, from that day they shall become free men and shall remain for ever free from the yoke of slavery". However, even prior to the year 1200 the force of these laws had become modified.

Membership of the Guilds

By that time legal opinion was largely that a serf, after residence in the town for the prescribed period of time '... if he should be received like a burgess into its common guild, will become liberated from serfdom by that very fact'. Thus it was membership of the guild, not the duration of residence, that became the essence of the law in such cases. This modification of the 'Willelmi Articuli' was reflected in most of the borough charters that were granted later than the year 1100.

Every town charter implied that the burgesses were willing to accept any outsider who showed a willingness to be a part of the borough and not a mere parasite on it. However, the burgesses were not concerned with quite the same aspects of the matter. It is true that serfs acquired some degree of freedom by mere residence in the town, so long as they remained therein, but when they wanted more than this, i.e. to be 'freeman' - not merely free men, they had to become members of the Guilds. Such membership was always difficult to attain, and sometimes it was totally impossible.

It was very hard for the serfs to cross the great gulf that existed between them and the burgesses. However, in London it was easier for a serf to obtain personal freedom because in the City's original charter granted by William the Conqueror the above quoted section of the 'Willelmi Articuli' was regarded as authoritative and could be successfully pleaded in the courts. Such freedom, however, was limited and gave no right of membership of a guild. A free birth was considered an essential condition of membership and the Guilds exercised a rigorous scrutiny over all applicants.

By 1300, birth in villeinage was generally regarded as tainting the blood. A City of London ordinance of 1387 laid down that no 'foreigner' should be enrolled as an apprentice unless he first swore that he was a free man and not a serf. Later a serf was defined as including the son of a man who was a serf at the time of the boy's birth. Therefore, if a villein became free by residence in the city, his sons born thereafter were eligible for membership of a guild. However, those born earlier were of servile origin and thus excluded. Similar obstacles existed in most cities and boroughs. Servile birth was either an absolute bar to membership or, at the very least, a licence by the relevant Lord was an essential requisite of a serf's admission.

The Roles of the Towns in Freeing the Serfs

The roles of the towns in the freeing of the serfs can be summarised thus:- The boroughs gave the fugitive serfs a great measure of protection against recapture by their Lords so long as they stayed within the town walls. However, their benevolence went no further than this and the advancement of the serfs was of little concern to the burgesses. Indeed, the majority of townsmen saw the landless serfs merely as convenient pools of casual labour. They used them as and when required then discarded them without assuming any responsibility for their welfare. Of course, there was a great demand for this casual labour in the medieval towns and the more highly organised the guilds became, the more the burgesses considered it beneath their dignity to carry out the day-to-day functions of town life.

This was where the fugitive serfs found their opportunity. They were employed doing a wide variety of labouring jobs as well as rough menial work in the houses of the merchants and tradesmen where they looked after the needs of the apprentices and journeymen. There was no end to the work to be done and many a fugitive serf must have felt that he had exchanged the service of his manorial Lord for that of a burgess.

Although in time the serfs became free of their manorial Lords, the towns must have seemed to them specially organised to prevent them from improving their conditions! The merchant guilds usually controlled the local government, and the craft guilds controlled all the worthwhile trades. As well as the full burgesses, there were various other privileged classes in the towns. For instance, the tenants and dependants of the Lords, Bishops, or Abbots, who lived within the Boroughs had certain trading rights and some 'foreigners,' who lived outside the walls, were licensed by the guilds to trade within them - 'according to the town's discretion and convenience.'

No doubt there were other class graduations. At the very bottom of the social structure were the ex-serfs without rights and with little chance of social advancement. To many of these runaways freedom in the towns amounted to little more than a choice between working and starving. However, a generation or two later their descendants were born freemen and burgesses, many becoming members of the guilds. Some made vast fortunes and even became aldermen, and mayors.

The Law and the Fugitive

Although there was a constant stream of desertions to the towns, the overwhelming majority of serfs were loath to leave their manorial holdings. Most Lords of the manor out of self-interest, if for no other reason, had found it was expedient to move with the times and conditions on the manors gradually improved and eventually approximated those enjoyed by the townsmen. The majority of serfs, therefore, considered their lives on the manors were not unduly harsh and were reluctant to leave them.

Those serfs who did desert the manors for the towns mostly did so out of desperation because their Lords, after all proper methods had been tried, were too reactionary, stupid, or grasping, to grant them greater freedom and better conditions. To such serfs as these, flight to the towns was the only means of advancement that was open to them.

Once a serf decided to run away it was very difficult for his Lords to restrain him. During the first four days of absence he could legally pursue the serf and re-take him, where-ever he was found. After that the Lords' powers of arrest were confined to their own manors, The deserter only had to remain hidden in the town for four days to gain sufficient protection to keep his Lord at bay. Thenceforth, if the Lord wanted to reclaim him he had to take legal action in the courts of common law. However, during this often lengthy procedure the serf often disappeared again!

The Lords did their utmost to keep their serfs on the manors. After all, each serf was a potential source of income to them and was not, therefore, lightly allowed to escape. The stewards constantly pronounced in the Manor Courts that it was the serf's duty to stay where they were. But it took more than words to stop them running away, and where the Lords had pre-knowledge that a serf was liable to desert various precautions were often taken. This usually took the form of selecting sureties to answer for the serf's good conduct and if the serf later deserted the manor the surety was liable to make good the Lord's losses. Sometimes a serf's relations were held responsible for his conduct and their land and goods were sequestered if he deserted the manor.

Sometimes, when the Lords found themselves powerless to prevent these desertions, they bowed to the inevitable and granted leaves of absence thereby retaining at least some appearance of authority! These permits were granted in return for a small payment called 'chevage,' to those wishing to live outside the manor. The sum involved was usually small, but the Lord usually added a proviso that the serf must come when called and attend the half-yearly Leet Courts.

In the small number of cases where leave of absence was given, it was publicly granted in the Manor Court, and details were duly recorded in the court rolls. This procedure served two purposes. Firstly, it gave official sanction to the serf's absence and, secondly, it impressed on the rest of the serfs that there was a right way of doing things! Regardless of such face-saving procedures a regular stream of discontented serfs deserted the manors. In many cases the Lords took no action to bring them back, probably feeling that it was not worth the expense and bother of chasing them, A more serious view was taken if the deserter was a villein with largish land holdings who owed service, because the loss of such a serf was a considerable blow to the manorial economy.

The King's Courts

In the latter circumstances the absentee was declared, by the Manor Court, to be a fugitive and he was ordered to return to the manor and any goods he left were sequestrated. Some times his fellow serfs were ordered to fetch the runaway back in time for the next court meeting on pain of fines for failure to do so. But such orders were of doubtful legality and were more or less unenforceable, and although they were repeated at subsequent Manor Court sessions, often for many years, they rarely resulted in the return of the absentees, nor were the fines ever inflicted. Once the deserters had been absent for four days, the Lord's only legal method of recovering their villeins was to seek the aid of the King's courts.

This step was not often taken because of the favourable attitude of the King's Courts towards runaway villeins. This was well expressed by Justice Herle, who said in 1309, ''In the beginning, every man in the world was free, and the law is so favourable to liberty that he who is once found free and of free estate in a court of record, shall be held to be free for ever unless it can be that some later act of his own makes him a villein.'' This quotation clearly indicates the difficulties facing the Lords when they resorted to the King's justices in order to recover their fugitive serfs. It may also explain why the Lords were reluctant to seek such aid unless the villein concerned was of sufficient value to the manorial economy to justify the costs involved!

Once the deserters had been absent for four days, the Lord's only legal method of recovering their villeins was to seek the aid of the King's Courts.

The King's Writ

The Lords' first step in the process of recovering a villein was to obtain the King's writ 'de nativo habendo.' This ordered the relevant Sheriff to deliver up the villein to his Lord, but only if he admitted that he was a villein. The serfs remedy therefore was to declare himself to be a free man and the Sheriff was powerless to seize him!

When the Sheriffs were thus prevented from executing the writ 'de nativo habendo,' the only way the Lords could proceed was to apply for a special writ which had the effect of removing the matter from the Sheriff's Court to the Royal Court so the case could be tried by the King's justices, either in London or on circuit. If the accused serf had the misfortune to be taken into custody by the accusing Lord, a powerful remedy was available to him by way of writ 'de homine replegiano.' Such a writ ordered the Sheriff to set the villein free from whosoever had custody of him. It also gave the Sheriff power to seize the custodian if he refused to obey the writ and to hold him until he complied. Once the serf had been produced and had provided adequate security to ensure his eventual appearance in court, the Sheriff released him until the pending charge of villeinage could be tried by the King's justices.

Another defence available to the serfs was the writ 'de liberate probanda.' This could be used by a man who feared his free status was in question and enabled him to clear his name of the slur of serfdom for all time by order of a court of record. The same writ could also be used by a man accused of being a serf and who had good reason to believe his accuser's evidence against him was insufficient. The effect of the writ was to stay all proceedings until the next coming of the circuit justices. When the case eventually came to court the accusing Lords were often under difficulties because of the growing belief of the Justices that 'judgement must be given in favour of liberty.'

Probing a Case

The onus was always on the Lord to prove his case and the accused serf was not even required to answer the charge unless the Lord, at the time of making his claim, produced at least two male witnesses who admitted their own villeinage and swore that they were related, by common ancestry, to the accused. Unless the Lord produced such evidence to the justice's complete satisfaction, the court decided in favour of the accused and declared him to be a free man for ever and the Lord was fined for false accusation!

In order to satisfy the justices it was essential that the kinsfolk produced as the accuser's witnesses were at least two in number and that they were all males. Females were considered too frail to stand as witnesses in such cases! The accused serfs were allowed to put up to three witnesses against their accuser, in spite of rules forbidding duplication in pleading.

As well as insisting on perfect presentation by the plaintiffs, the courts favoured those who sought liberty in every way they could. For example, if the plaintiff's witnesses refused to give evidence, were females, or were too distantly related to the accused, the law assumed the plaintiff had no proper witnesses and declared the accused to be a free man for ever. The law refused to assume that a bastard, being an illegal son, was a serf merely because of the unfree status of his natural father. But it was always assumed that a stranger who had settled on manorial land was a free man and the law refused to construe any uncertainty regarding his status. The justices freely allowed those accused of serfdom to take advantage of any mistakes in pleading, or technical errors of presentation, in their accusers' case. A clever attorney, therefore, could find many opportunities to make life difficult for the Lords in their actions against alleged serfs!

It is unlikely those serfs who resorted to the courts were representative of their class. It required brains, money and courage to set the medieval lawyers in motion and only a very few serfs would have had the means or pluck to attempt it. Such action meant delay until the itinerant justices came. It also meant the employment of an attorney and the production of the necessary witnesses etc.

It is fairly certain that only a few serfs would have had the temerity to take their cases to the King's courts of common law. Those few who did so deserved all the help a tolerant judge could give them! But however favourable towards the serfs the courts were, the law could never deny the rights of a Lord over his serf if such rights were properly presented in the courts.

The records seem to imply that the Lords' most common motive for taking wayward serfs to court was to establish their servile status for all time. In the courts the serfs were usually so intimidated by their surroundings they put up little or no fight. In the majority of cases the accused serf had little or no defence against the Lord's charges and was soon forced to acknowledge his status. This was final for an admission made in a court of record could always be appealed to and once the peasant had admitted his serfdom his hopes of freedom were gone for ever!

It was always assumed that a stranger who had settled on manorial land was a free man and the law refused to construe any uncertainty regarding his status.

For those men who were forced to admit their status the law could do nothing. However, if a man put up some show of defence everything that the law could use in his favour was used. It should not be assumed that the Lords always lost these cases. In fact from records they seem to have been successful about three times out of four.

It would appear that most Lords took great care in getting their evidence together and usually presented very strong cases to the courts. There are examples of Lords failing to prosecute when their cases eventually came to court. The comparative frequency of such cases seems to indicate that Lords sometimes used the writs to intimidate the serfs into returning to the manors, thus saving themselves the uncertainty, expense and anxiety of going to court. When these tactics failed, the Lords appear to have lost interest, defaulted, and gave up all claims. Those they accused were declared by the court to be free men and the Lords concerned were fined for false accusation. The Sheriffs, in such circumstances, were ordered to insure that the relevant defendants were not subjected to future harassment by the Lords.

The courts in the fourteenth century made it more and more clear that serfdom was repugnant to the law of England. The general, if gradual, movement towards personal freedom continued until, by the year 1600, there were no serfs in the Kingdom. The contributing factors were many and varied; the harshness of overlords; the attraction of the towns; and the growing realisation that forced labour was less profitable that hired labour. Other major causes were the results of war, famine, and plague. These three factors depleted the manorial population and left Lords with vacant land holdings they were only too glad to let for money rent, sooner that servile dues. All these things, together with new farming methods and other causes, finally brought the feudal system of servile land holdings to an end. With it came the end of the personal subjection of Englishmen and all its humiliating consequences.

The Church and the Manor

In medieval times the church had great prestige and authority over the lives of all men including manorial serfs. The church building itself usually stood in the centre of the village, thus symbolising its central place in medieval life. All the most significant moments of life - baptism, marriage and death - centred on the sacred building. Therein the peasants heard the mass on Sundays and learnt about religion from the pictures and carvings on the walls, and the sermons of the village priests or the itinerant friars.

To the medieval peasants, religion was not just for Sundays, nor were their lives divided between religious and secular matters. In fact the church was an omnipresent part of their daily routine. They felt its influence in their fields, closes and asarts, and as they went about the manor they saw the wayside crosses and local shrines where, from time immemorial, prayers had been said and offerings made. There was also a constant stream of wandering friars, ecclesiastics on business, and groups of pilgrims, visiting or passing through the villages.

Religion was so very much a part of normal everyday medieval life that the vast majority of peasants were believers, even if some of them were less than enthusiastic about it! To be a declared unbeliever or a heretic in those days was a rare and unenviable situation, and so most people conformed. Those who did not were outcasts and they were made to feel their exile by every available means. Most men undoubtedly feared such isolation, but were well aware that they were liable to suffer much more than mere loneliness if the church took action against them.

The medieval church was a militant organisation and its contacts with the peasants were not solely those of love and compassion! When the church's rights or dues were threatened the lay Lords of the Manor were quick to take its side. The tithe barn was a constant reminder to the peasants of the church's power and needs and the payment of tithes, mortuaries, and various other church dues were ruthlessly exacted from them.

On top of this the village priest was often in direct competition with the serfs in agricultural matters. They were usually priests first and farmers second, but it was not unknown for them to put their profits as farmers first! The priests' animals competed for food with those of their parishioners on the common, and the priests bargained against the serfs in the local markets, often undercutting and outbidding them. However, the church's power over the peasantry was backed up by even more powerful, but invisible, forces.

These forces were constantly at work on the peasants' consciences and were largely induced by the fearsome sermons of the priests and reinforced by the paintings and carvings that adorned the church. Their theme was the notion of a last judgement followed either by salvation of eternal Hell-fire! The church taught that a soul, even at death, could be saved. Therefore, not surprisingly, men became obsessed with the idea of death and the preparation for it.

The Power of the Devil

The benign shadow of the cross covered the medieval peasants' world: but there was also another, more sinister, shadow which darkened their lives and thoughts - the fear of the devil and all his works. This was no mere conjecture so far as the peasants were concerned, they were fully convinced that every corner of their homes and fields was liable to harbour some agent of Hell who could cause them real hurt unless it was exorcised and overcome.

From the earliest times, the church had needed to accommodate many old pagan customs and legends which it could not stamp out. It dealt with these by the simple method of giving them Christian interpretations. Wells, springs and other places, which had once been dedicated to pagan gods, were consecrated, re-named and placed under the patronage of Christian Saints.

The pagan celebrations of Midsummer on the 21st of June were postponed by the Christians until the eve of the feast of St. John the Baptist on the 23rd of June. It was then observed by dancing and the lighting of bonfires. So the pagan festival survived.

Many of the pagan rites that were associated with the agricultural seasons were absorbed into the Christian calendar. These pagan rites were adapted to reflect a Christian message. For example, the Harvest Festival is almost entirely pagan in origin. It was originally called Lammas, meaning "Loafmas," and was celebrated on the 1st of August. In more recent times it has become a movable festival, timed to suit local seasonal variations from year to year.

The Parish Priest

Most medieval parish priests were of peasant stock and were usually taught, the little they knew, by older peasant priests. This had the disadvantage of perpetuating the ignorance and superstition of the clergy.

In the year 1281, Archbishop Pecham is on record as saying 'The ignorance of the priests casteth the people into the ditch of error,' and similar sentiments were still being expressed three centuries later by Cardinal Wolsey. Clerical ignorance was so widespread that most peasants learnt little or nothing of the deeper meaning of religion from their village priests.

By and large the medieval priests were far from being the kindly, cultured, patrons of village life that the parsons of the last two centuries have so often been. They were more likely to have been hardened men of business. They were often strangers brought into villages from outside by bribery of, or influence over, the church hierarchy. Often they had little in common with their parishioners except a determination to overcome the difficulties of medieval agriculture, and an eye for a bargain.

The Priest's Stipends

In most cases the parish priests received stipends from the church which were worth about twice the contemporary wages earned by skilled farm workers, such as ploughmen. Thus the social status of the average priest equalled that of the better off villeins - the thirty acre men.

However, the priests' stipends had to support not only themselves and any minor clerics who assisted them, but also their 'hearth-mates' - the women who tended their households and no doubt their other needs!

Many parish priests found it impossible to exist on their stipends alone and had to engage in agriculture. Practically all parish priests had a certain amount of land called 'the glebe,' assigned to them in the manors by virtue of their office. This 'glebe land' was either cultivated by the parsons themselves, or rented out to others. These 'church furlongs' or 'parson's closes,' as they were called, encouraged the clergy to take part in the agricultural life of the manors.

Thus the clergy were forced to enter into open competition with their parishioners for the sale of surplus stock and crops, and indulge in the buying and selling of produce and livestock which was against church law. Although the church constantly issued rebukes regarding these practices it totally failed to eliminate them.

The involvement of the clergy in agriculture inevitably resulted in disputes between the priests and peasants which ended up in the Manor Courts. Manorial records show many instances of priests being rebuked and fined for offences against manorial customs or for infringing other mens' rights.

By and large the medieval priests were far from being the kindly, cultured, patrons of village life that the parsons of the last two centuries have so often been.

This did little to improve their religious authority over their congregations! Business interests and religious principles were fundamentally incompatible and much ill feeling between priests and peasants originated in the manorial fields and market-places.

Mortuary

There was also another source of much friction and ill will between the priests and their flock. With the Lord's right to demand 'heriots' went a sinister claim by the church called 'mortuary.' This was levied on the estate of a serf after their death and usually consisted of a claim on the second best beast which was chosen by the parish priest immediately after the Lord had selected his 'heriot.'

The church justified this imposition in Canon Law, on the grounds that the dead serf had probably underpaid his 'tithes' during his lifetime! However, the Canon Law did have the grace to prohibit the taking of a 'mortuary' unless the peasant died possessed of at least three beasts.

The imposition of 'heriot' and 'mortuary,' like most similar burdens, became regulated and modified by manorial custom. On some manors they were exacted with extreme harshness, on others with merciful consideration. However, in general they were cruel extortions which, by their very nature, were demanded at times of maximum sorrow and distress. In some instances the Lord of the Manor and the church were one and the same entity. There are many records of the serf's families being deprived of the best two thirds of their meagre possessions by Abbots, Abbesses, Bishops and other ecclesiastical officers - presumably these worthies were not too troubled by their 'Christian' consciences.

Tithes

Tithes were of ancient origin and had the full sanction of ecclesiastical law and were thus binding on all men. The system had been used since early Christian times to provide revenue for the upkeep of the church and clergy. Basically the system demanded that one tenth part of all agricultural produce be handed over to the parish priest.

The system survived, much modified, until it finally phased out in 1936. Throughout it's long history men paid tithes very reluctantly and they resented the church for exacting them. To most men, especially the poorer serfs with the smallest holdings, it seemed unreasonable that the church should take part of their meagre harvests and give it to a man who was comparatively well-to-do. The church did nothing to help explain matters. In the severest manner it laid down what items were tithable and it most rigorously insisted on their full payment.

In addition to their main tithes, which were taken from the grain and fodder yields, tithes were also demanded from a wide range of other agricultural products.

The church defined, in considerable detail, exactly what items of production were tithable and also demanded its ten per cent of the meat of all slaughtered beasts and poultry; eggs; honey; milk; butter and cheese; and from the wool yield - which the church held to include even the down from ducks and geese.

Tithes were also claimed on the pot-herbs and fruit that the serfs grew in their closes and from the wild fruits, nuts, herbs and reeds etc., that they gathered from the woodlands. The church even took a tenth part of the grass the serfs cut from the road sides.

The Church was pitiless in the demands it made, especially on the poorer peasants. Tithes, taken together with the church's right to claim mortuaries, amounted to a complete system of income tax, land tax, and death duties! It was a far more onerous set of taxes that anything known today - and it was unpopular in direct proportion to its severity.

Without doubt the tithes were a very important source of income to the church. It is not surprising that they were exacted with considerable pressure where such was necessary. Chaucer says of his idealised parish priest, 'Full loath were him to cursen for his tithes,' but such godly clerics were, in practice, very rare.

The church reserved its very fiercest curses for those who resisted its authority in these matters and the parish priests were instructed to pronounce the excommunication with bell, book and candle, of all those who dared to withhold their tithes.

It is not surprising that the continuous demands for tithe, rigorously enforced as it was, led to many difficulties and often tended to estrange the priests from their flocks. The peasants could not understand why they should be forced to make these payments to a man, although a priest, who was of their own class and worked in the fields just as they did themselves.

The Church was pitiless in the demands it made, especially on the poorer peasants.

The peasants, quite naturally, resented being compelled to give part of their hard won produce to the priests, especially when the glebe lands that were granted to the clergy by virtue of their holy orders, were among the largest and richest of the manorial holdings. Where the tithes were more than enough to maintain the priest and the parish church, the surplus was given to the Cathedrals and Monasteries and often found its way into secular hands which caused further discontent.

The English tithe system lasted a very long time. It is first mentioned by the Venerable Bede, c677-735AD, and in 750AD Egbert, Archbishop of York, instructed his clergy 'to teach the people to pay tithes.'

The rise of the various dissenting religions in the eighteenth and nineteenth centuries gave rise to much agitating, and many people were imprisoned for non-payment of their tithes. Under the Tithes Commutation Act 1836, payment in kind was replaced by perpetual, annual rent charges, assessed on corn values. In 1925 provisions were made to abolish tithes altogether, and in 1936 the tithe rents were replaced by annuities, which were redeemable over a period of time, and are now extinct.

The Decline of the Manorial System

The manorial elements of serfdom and bondage were Anglo Saxon in origin and the feudal aspects of military obligations and seigniorial powers were introduced later by the Normans. In practice, these two features were incapable of separation but, when observing the break up of the medieval system, it is convenient to treat them separately because both the causes and rate of change were different in each case.

There were three main types of feudal land tenure - two military and one ecclesiastical. The most honourable type of military tenure was 'Sergeantry,' which was held in return for some personal service rendered to the King. However, the majority of military tenures were held in 'Knights service,' which obliged the holder to train and arm a number of knights and lead them in military service under the King's command for forty days in each year. The non-military tenures were held in 'Frankalmoign' (free alms) by the church in return for the performance of their religious duties.

King Henry II ruled from 1154 to 1189, and towards the end of his reign he enacted a series of laws known as the Assize of Arms 1181. These laws, which foreshadowed the eventual break up of the feudal system, were intended to curb the barons' misuse of their powers to raise armies. During his reign the feudal armies, composed of the barons and their retainers, had proved to be unreliable, inefficient and liable to be used in rebellion against him. By his legislation, Henry sought to counterbalance the latter situation by reviving the ancient Anglo Saxon principle of universal military service to provide the national forces.

The Assize of Arms 1181, therefore, decreed that all free men must provide themselves with armour and weapons commensurate to their status and wealth. The sheriffs, acting under the justices, were required to see that the provisions of these laws were enforced and to call up and lead the local forces, or 'shire levy,' in times of emergency. King Henry II also encouraged his barons to opt out of the irksome military burden of 'knight service' by paying, in lieu thereof, a monetary tax called 'scutage,' meaning shield money. The 'scutage' thus collected was used by the King to pay for a standing army of professional soldiers.

After the middle of the thirteenth century the role of heavily armoured knights in warfare gradually decreased and the need for infantry and archers led by mounted officers increased. By 1327 English knights were being trained to fight on foot, as well as on horseback, and a new class of professional officer grew up. As the years passed 'knight service' tenure became obsolete and payment of 'scutage' became the norm.

By the Statute of Winchester in 1285, King Edward I extended the scope of the Assize of Arms so as to include all men aged 16 to 60, whether free or serf. He appointed a Commissioner of Array in every English County who was required to produce a 'muster roll' containing the name of, and type of arms held by, every man in his County and mobilise them in time of war.

Thus the effects of 'scutage,' Assize of Arms, and the shire levy, caused the old feudal land burdens gradually to dissolve. Ever since the Crown had introduced the custom of employing professional soldiers instead of relying on feudal 'knight services,' the nobles and great barons had sought to follow the example of the Kings and covenants in which small land holders agreed to serve their powerful neighbours in arms - 'except against the King' - became commonplace. However, the latter restriction was not always observed and the old feudal bonds of mutual loyalty grew ever weaker.

The Demise of the Manor

The major cause of the eventual demise of the medieval manorial system was the gradual achievement of free status by the serfs. Other principle causes were the effects of the Statute of Merton of 1235; the Lords' preference for employing free workers on their demesne lands as opposed to relying of the compulsory services of unwilling serfs; and the shortage of labour created by the Black Death of 1348. Gradually quit rents, which the Lords used to pay their workers, replaced the compulsory work services of the serfs, and contracts between landlord and tenant replaced villeinage and strict adherence to the 'customs of the manor.'

The Statute of Merton in 1235 permitted the Lords of the Manor to enclose pieces of manorial wasteland. However, there was a proviso that enough of such wasteland must remain open to sustain the peasants' various rights of common. This resulted in pieces of common land being enclosed and sold, purely for the Lord's personal profit. The purchasers of such land not being restricted by 'custom of the manor' were free to develop new and more efficient methods of farming. These land sales were completed with due formality in the Manorial Courts and details of the contracts of purchase, including any rights or obligations entered into by the parties, were recorded in the manorial rolls. The only proof of title such purchasers ever had was a copy of the relevant entry in the court rolls, and they therefore became known as copyholders.

The payment of quit rents in lieu of work services was mutually beneficial to both the serfs and the Lords. The only way the peasants could raise the quit rents was by the sale of surplus crops. However, the contemporary farming methods, whereby the peasants cultivated widely scattered strips of land, were too inefficient to enable them to produce enough surplus crops to sell.

The Enclosure of the Common Fields

One way in which the Lords overcame this impasse, to everybody's satisfaction, was to enclose the 'common fields' - not to be confused with the enclosures of open common land. After enclosure, the common fields were cultivated communally and the customary strip system became defunct. This resulted in greatly increased agricultural production because the peasants spent less time travelling between the widely scattered strips, thus enabling fewer met to produce bigger harvests. Secondly, the raised baulks of land between strips became redundant and were therefore ploughed up, thus increasing the land area under cultivation. The enlarged harvests thus produced were capable of feeding the peasants and also produced enough surplus crops to be sold in order to pay a communal quit rent to the Lord of the Manor.

The latter procedure worked well enough where the manorial holdings were of fairly equal size. Where this was the case, the Lords divided the common fields amongst the villeins in proportion to the number of strips they each cultivated. This resulted in the creation of a number of closed farms of various sizes. Details of the tenants, conditions of tenure, and the quit rents payable, for these new farms were duly entered into the manorial rolls, and the customary rights of common and pasture were usually re-confined. Thus the erstwhile villeins effectively became copyholders and they were free to cultivate their farms however they wished, so long as they paid their rents. The wasteful strip system was abandoned and the peasants' new found freedom enabled them to experiment and innovate new farming methods that enabled them to produce surplus crops which they sold in order to pay their quit rents.

The change to closed field farming, which had started in a small way after 1236, continued over many years and gradually replaced the wasteful cultivation of open field strips. By the year 1700 this change over was almost complete. However, a few open field farms survived even into the first half of the twentieth century. These enclosures of the communal fields, when done by mutual agreement, were beneficial to Lords and peasants alike. They were also an essential prerequisite to the advance of agriculture. The latter enclosures should not be confused with the enclosures of commons and pastures by the Lords purely for profit, which caused so many evictions, hardships and losses of rights of common for the peasants, usually without adequate compensation.

Such enclosures, made to create freehold and copyhold farms to sell for profit, continued to be made and the movement reached its peak between 1700 and 1845. After around 1700, such enclosures were made by special Acts of Parliament, usually promoted by the Lords in order to legalise their own actions. These Acts distributed the common lands between the Lords of the manor and those to whom they had sold them. Four thousand such Acts were passed during the period 1700-1845 under which 5,000,000 acres of common land were enclosed.

An Act of 1801 decreed that three-quarters of the existing freeholders and copyholders on a manor must agree to any proposed enclosures thereof. In 1845 a commission was appointed to examine all proposed enclosures and to ensure that in any given case enough common land remained in public use. At about the same time the movement for the preservation of the commons came into being and many proposed enclosures were prevented, an example of which was Epping Forest. An Act of 1876 stopped all further enclosures of common land. By then it was too late because practically all such land, if capable of cultivation, had already been enclosed.

The Effect of the Black Death

The ravages of the Black Death, which swept the land in 1348, accelerated the break up of the medieval manors. This terrible plague, which killed off at least a third of the population, caused a great labour shortage and rising wages. Serfs deserted their manors in droves and, by presenting themselves as free men, found ready employment on nearby manors at higher wages and with few questions asked about their status. These serfs eventually became free men by 'possession.' The high death rate and desertions from the manors created a lively market in vacant and abandoned farms and copyhold tenure became more widespread.

To overcome the labour shortage Lords of the Manor changed from arable farming to the much less labour intensive sheep farming which was becoming even more profitable. This was achieved by enclosing vast areas of common and wasteland. This was done ruthlessly and often to the detriment of the peasantry, many of whom suffered eviction and either starved or joined the vast army of vagabonds who terrorised the countryside. By 1600 as many as 50,000 evictions had taken place due to such enclosures. Even if they escaped eviction the peasants suffered great hardships from loss of grazing and other rights of common because of the Lords' greed.

The 1351 Statute of Labourers, which sought to fix wages at their 1346 level, augmented the seething discontent of the peasantry. But it was the imposition of a poll tax in 1377 that proved to be the last straw and resulted in the Peasants' revolt of 1381. This was ruthlessly suppressed and harsh reprisals were taken which only helped swell the already existing army of wandering vagabonds.

Due to the various causes already discussed, serfdom eventually gave way to freedom. It has to be said in passing that for some people 'freedom' amounted to little more than a choice between working and starving, or turning to crime and getting hung if caught! However, there is no actual point in time at which it could be said that the medieval system ended. The process was more evolutionary than revolutionary. The only known facts are that in 1350 half of the population of England were villeins and two hundred and fifty years later there were no villeins left in the Kingdom. Thus serfdom, the very essence of the medieval manorial system, which had for so long been repugnant in English law, just simply died out.

INDEX